Pass the Numerical Reasoning Test

GW00788711

By Vali Nasser

ISBN-13: 978-1489523983

ISBN-10: 1489523987

2nd version Feb 2014

Every effort has been made by the author to ensure that the material in this book is up to date and in line with the requirements to pass various types of numeracy reasoning tests at the time of publication. The author will also do his best to review, revise and update this material periodically as necessary. However, neither the author nor the publisher can accept responsibility for loss or damage resulting from the material in this book

About the Author

The author of this book has experience in both consultancy work and teaching.

The author's initial book 'Speed Mathematics Using the Vedic System' has a significant following and has been translated into Japanese and Chinese as well as German. In addition, his book 'Pass the QTS Numeracy test with ease' is very popular with teacher trainees.

Besides being a specialist mathematics teacher the author also has a degree in psychology. This has enabled him to work as an organizational development consultant giving him exposure to psychometric testing particularly applicable to numerical reasoning. Besides working in consultancy he also managed the QTS numeracy tests for teacher trainees at OCR in conjunction with the teaching agency. Subsequently he has tutored and taught mathematics and statistics in schools as well as in adult education.

He hopes that his new book 'Pass the Numerical reasoning Test with Ease' will help those aspiring to pass basic, intermediate as well as advanced numeracy tests when applying for jobs in various sectors of the economy.

For consulting companies, large multinationals as well as the banking and financial sector you will probably need to get fairly high marks and work to tighter time scales in the appropriate numerical reasoning tests. Some guidelines on the marks required are given during the practice tests in this book.

Introduction

This book is aimed at helping you pass the intermediate and advanced numerical reasoning tests that many companies now require for new or experienced graduates wanting to progress in their professional careers. If you feel that you need to improve your speed in the Mental Arithmetic part of the test and re-visit some areas in general arithmetic as well as data interpretation then this book will prove very useful to you. It will be particularly helpful if you do not feel very confident in maths, or did your maths a long time ago. The questions in the aptitude tests of numerical reasoning come in a variety of forms. Basic questions may involve simple multiplication, working out percentages, ratios, proportions and number sequences. Multiple choice questions are usually found in the data interpretation type questions. In addition, for some tests you may need to be familiar with basic algebra such as converting a temperature from Fahrenheit to Celsius, or working out the time taken, given the distance and the speed using the appropriate formula as necessary. Usually the formula in the context of the question is given. Finally, in word problems the use of simple algebra can be very useful in solving the questions set.

Just for your information, research has shown that numerical aptitude tests correlate well with performance as well as future growth prospects so more and more companies use these tests in addition to your interview and other aptitude tests that you may be given.

This book covers the type of questions that you are likely to meet in an aptitude test consisting of numerical reasoning questions both at an intermediate and advanced level.

Advanced numerical tests are not to be confused with advanced mathematics. You don't need complex algebra or calculus to do these questions but you do need to be familiar with basics such as converting from one currency into another given an exchange rate, or be familiar with working out compound interest rates. In addition, you are expected to know how to manipulate fractions, decimals and percentages of quantities similar to basic numeracy but typically the questions in advanced tests will require you to perform more steps before reaching an answer. Also you need to be able to work more quickly. In some tests one minute per question is not uncommon. Multiple choice questions are also quite popular particularly those involving data interpretation. In addition, you will be set more complex problems which involve time, money, proportion and ratio, percentages, fractions and decimals, measurements, conversions and averages, including mean, median, mode and range, bar and line charts and cumulative frequency charts where relevant. Most of the examples in the statistics or data interpretation section given are those that you are expected to be familiar with when working for large corporations. In addition a practice test with multiple choice questions is also given.

Although a lot of the material in the first two chapters will be familiar to you, hopefully you will find some of the 'Speed Methods' introduced helpful for working out basic questions in arithmetic quickly. This will help you to work within tight time frames.

One thing to remember is there is often more than one way of working out a given problem. It does not matter which method you use, so long as you feel comfortable with it. You will be marked only for the correct answer. The arithmetic part of the book gives you a variety of methods to choose from, including 'Speed Methods' of calculations.

Finally, although some of you may find the first two chapters very easy and be tempted to skip them, my advice is to go through them quickly to make sure you remind yourself of speed methods of adding and subtracting as well as those of multiplying and dividing without a calculator. Remember in the actual test you will be working against limited time. Good luck with your tests.

Further details on numerical reasoning tests can be found from SHL and PSL/Kenexa some of the biggest providers of psychometric tests. In addition, web addresses of sample tests from the Civil Service as well as Kent University are also given at the end of this book.

Chapter 1:   Arithmetic part I

Addition and Subtraction using Speed Methods

The normal approach of column addition and subtraction is a good method and if you feel happy with it then you should have no problems with this part of arithmetic. Make sure that when dealing with adding and subtracting decimal numbers, the decimal points are aligned.

The following additional methods will prove useful in increasing your speed which could be a critical part of many numerical reasoning tests

Consider the *Speed Method* below for addition

Compensating or adjusting method

In this method we simply adjust by adding or subtracting from the rounded up or rounded down number as shown in the examples below. In example1 we round up 96 to 100 and adjust by taking away 4. Similarly we round up 69 to 70 and adjust by taking away 1. See below for all the working out.

Example 1:

$96 + 69 =$

$100 - 4 + 70 - 1 =$

$170 - 5 = 165$

Example 2:

$59 + 88 + 23 =$

$60 - 1 + 90 - 2 + 20 + 3 =$

$150 + 20 - 3 + 3 = 170$

Basic Arithmetic Question

A customer buys three items from a shoe shop, items A, B and C. The selling prices are as follows: A sells for £23.90, B sells for £33.75 and C sells for £19.95. A customer buys all three items. Find the total amount the customer has to pay.

Method:

Total cost = £23.90 + £33.75 +£19.95

= £24 - 10p +£34 - 25p + £20 – 5p = £24 +£34 +£20 - 10p - 25p - 5p

= £78 – 40p = £77.60

Subtraction

You probably remember column subtraction and the number line method from your GCSE days or from when you last did maths. Before we go on to use the *'Speed Method'* let us revisit the familiar method for subtraction.

Example :

Work out: 241 - 28

Traditional column method

The traditional methods of subtraction serve us well in mathematics. However, there is one more strategy that we can use to make this process much easier but more of this later. First we will consider the normal approach.

Consider the following example:

$$241$$
$$-\quad 28$$
$$\overline{}$$
$$213$$
$$\overline{}$$

Starting from the right hand side we cannot subtract 8 from 1 so we borrow 1 from the tens column to make the units column 11. Subtracting 8 from 11 gives us 3, however since we have taken away 1 from the tens column we are left with 3 in this column. Subtracting 2 from 3 in the tens column gives us 1. Since we have nothing else to take away the final answer is 213.

Speed Method of Subtraction

Example 1: Now consider the same problem using a *Speed Method*.

If we add 2 to the top and bottom number we get:

$$243 \quad (241+2)$$

$$- \quad 30 \quad (28+2)$$

$$\underline{213}$$

You can see that subtracting 30 from 243 is easier than subtracting 28 from 241!

This strategy relies on the algebraic fact that if you add or subtract the same number from the top and bottom numbers you do not change the answer to the subtraction sum.

So essentially we try and add or subtract a certain number to both the numbers in order to make the sum simpler. A few more examples will help.

Example 2:

$$113$$

$$- \, 6$$

$$\underline{}$$

Add 4 to both numbers (we want to try to make the units column 0 in the bottom row if we can and if it helps) So the new sum is:

$$117$$

$$- 10$$

$$\overline{}$$

$$107$$

$$\overline{}$$

We can see that if we subtract 10 from 117 we get 107.

Example 3:

$$321$$

$$\underline{- 114}$$

Let us add 6 to each number so that the unit column in the bottom number becomes a 0 as shown below:

$$327 \text{ (add 6 to 321)}$$

$$\underline{- 120} \text{ (add 6 to 114)}$$

$$\underline{207}$$

Subtracting 120 from 327 we get 207 as shown. No borrowing is required.

Note: Sometimes you might find the method above useful; at other times it is easier to revert to the traditional method.

Subtracting from 100, 1000, 10000, 100000

Some people find subtracting from 1000, 10000 or 100000 difficult, so let us consider a useful technique for doing this.

Subtracting from 100, 1000 or 10000 using a '*Speed Method*'

In this case we use the rule **'all from nine and the last from 10'**

Example 1: 100 -76

We simply take each figure (except the last) in 76 from 9 and the last from 10 as shown below:

$$
\begin{array}{r}
1\,0\,0 \\
-\ \ 76 \\
\hline
2\,4 \\
\hline
\end{array}
$$

Take 7 from 9 to give 2 and take 6 from 10 to give 4

Example 2: 1000 – 897 =103

We simply take each figure (except the last) in 897 from 9 and the last from 10 as shown below:

$$
\begin{array}{r}
1\,0\,0\,0 \\
-\,8\,9\,7 \\
\hline
1\,0\,3 \\
\hline
\end{array}
$$

(Take 8 from 9 to give 1. Take 9 from 9 to give 0 and take 7 from 10 to give 3)

Subtracting from 2000, 3000, 4000, 5000, or more thousands

From the above, use the principle of 'last from 10 and the rest from nine' and 'subtracting 1 from the first digit on the left after all the zeros'

Example 1: Work out 3000 – 347

Using the principle of 'last from 10 the rest from nine' and 'subtracting 1 from the first digit on the left after all the zeros'.

We get the answer to be 2653

Example 2: Work out 7000 − 462

Similarly, the answer in this case is 6538.

Typical Question

At a pharmaceutical company a scientist has 10000 Milliliters of a particular liquid which she uses for her experiments. She uses up 8743 Milliliters after several experimental tests. How much does she have left?

Method:

$$1\,0\,0\,0\,0$$

$$-\,8\,7\,4\,3$$

$$\underline{1\,2\,5\,7}$$

(Take 8 from 9 to give 1, 7 from 9 to give 2, 4 from 9 to give 5 and finally 3 from 10 to give 7)

This means the scientist has 1257 milliliters of liquid left.

Multiplying & Dividing by 10, 100 and 1000 (by powers of 10)

You are expected to be familiar with multiplying and dividing numbers by 10, 100, 1000 or any other power of 10

Speed Method: Rule for multiplying whole numbers:

(1) When multiplying a whole number by 10 add a zero at the end of the number.

(2) When multiplying by 100 add two zeros.

(3) When multiplying by 1000 add three zeros

(4) You simply add the number of zeros reflected in the power of 10.

Some examples will illustrate this:

(1) 45 X 10 =450 (add 1 zero to 45)

(2) 67 X 100=6700 (add 2 zeros to 67)

(3) 65 X 1000=65000 (add 3 zeros to 65)

(4) 65788 X 1000000 = 65788000000 (add 6 zeros to 65788)

Speed Method: Rules for numbers with decimals:

When multiplying by 10, 100, 1000 move the decimal place the appropriate number of places to the right.

(1) 67.5 X 10 =675 (the decimal point is moved 1 place to the right to give us 675.0 which is the same as 675)

(2) 67.5 X 100 =6750 (this time move the decimal point two places to the right to give 6750.0 which is the same as 6750)

(3) 6.87 X 1000 =6870 (in this case move the decimal point three places to the right to give the required answer.)

Now consider examples involving division by 10, 100 and 1000 and other powers of ten.

(1) 450 ÷ 10 = 45 (You simply remove one zero from the number)

(2) 5600 ÷ 100 =56 (This time you remove two zeros from the number)

(3) 45 ÷ 100=0.45 (No zeros to remove – so this time move the decimal point two places to the left to give us 0.45)

(4) 345.78 ÷ 100 =3.4578 (Again simply move the decimal point 2 places to the left to give the answer)

(5) 456.78 ÷ 1000 =0.45678 (Move the decimal point 3 places to the left as shown)

(6) 458 ÷ 0.1 =4580 (remember 0.1 means one–tenth, so dividing a number by 0.1 or one-tenth means the answer becomes 10 times bigger.)

Questions involving powers of 10

(1) Divide 27000 Milliliters by 100

(2) What is78.87 multiplied by 1000?

(3) What is 67 divided by 100?

(4) What is 687 divided by 0.1? (Tip: Dividing by 0.1 is the same as dividing by one tenth, the answer should thus be 10× bigger))

Using the methods shown earlier the answers are:

(1) 270 ml   (2) 78870 (3) 0.67 (4) 6870

If you feel comfortable with the methods above you can skip the traditional method below - although if you have time it will add to your conceptual understanding and will help explain why the 'speed method' leads to the correct answers. If you decide to skip the next bit make sure you look at the last part to do with large and small numbers.

Traditional method of multiplying by 10

The traditional method of multiplying by a 10, 100, 1000 is shown below. This method is useful as it cements the conceptual understanding required. Consider having to work out 34 × 10

Consider place value. For example for the number 34, the right hand digit is the units digit and the number 3 on the left hand side is the tens digit or column. In fact every time you move one place to the left you increase the value by 10. So moving left by one place from the tens column we get the 100's column as shown below.

Hundreds	Tens	Units
	3	4

When we multiply by 10 each digit moves one column to the left. So 34 × 10 =340 as shown below. In other words 3 tens becomes 3 hundreds, the 4 units becomes 4 tens as shown. Also notice we have 0 units so we must put a zero in the units column. Moving each digit 1 place to the left has the effect of making it 10 × bigger.

Hundreds	Tens	Units
3	4	0

Consider the sum 34 × 100

Multiplying by 100 is similar. We simply multiply by 10 and then 10 again. This has the effect of moving each digit two places to the left. This makes it 100 × bigger.

The number 34 is shown below as 3 tens and 4 units.

Thousands	Hundreds	Tens	Units
		3	4

We will now do the multiplication and see its effect.

Clearly multiplying 34 by 100 has the effect of moving the 3 in the tens column to the thousands column and the 4 units to the hundreds column. This is shown below.

Thousands	Hundreds	Tens	Units
3	4	0	0

So 34 × 100 = 3400 as shown above.

This technique is important as it illustrates the concept of multiplying by 10 or 100 taking place. The same process applies to multiplying by 1000, 10,000 or a higher power of 10.

Also note, there is a short hand way of writing 100, 1000, 10,000 and larger powers of 10.

$100 = 10^2$ (10 squared, which is 10 X 10)

$1000 = 10^3$ (10 cubed which is 10 X 10 X 10)

$10,000 = 10^4$ ((10 to the power 4, which is 10 X 10 X 10 X 10)

$1000,000 = 10^6$ (10 to the power 6 which is 10 X 10 X 10 X 10 X 10 X 10)

Higher powers can be written similarly.

Large numbers:

These days it is conventional to use the USA system for billion and trillion.

A million is 1000000 or 10^6

A billion is a thousand million which is 1000,000,000 or 10^9

A trillion is a thousand billion which is 1000,000,000,000 or 10^{12}

(In the traditional British system although the number for a million is the same as the American system, it is different for a billion and trillion. In the traditional UK system a billion is a million, million or 10^{12} and a trillion is a million, million, million or 10^{18})

The US system is now typically used in finance and in Industry.

Small numbers:

One tenth is $\frac{1}{10}$ = 0.1 but can also be written 10^{-1}

One hundredth $=\frac{1}{100}$ =0.01 which can be written as 10^{-2}

One thousandth $=\frac{1}{1000}$ =0.001 which can be written as 10^{-3}

One millionth $= \frac{1}{1000000}$ =0.000001 which can be written as 10^{-6}

Any small number can be written as power of 10 with a negative sign as shown above. Very small numbers are useful in science, for example in particle physics.

Dividing by 10, 100 and 1000

Conceptually, dividing by 10, 100 or 1000 is a similar process, except, on this occasion, you move the digits to the right by the appropriate number of places.

Consider having to divide 34 by 10.

Here 3 tens and 4 units becomes 3 units and 4 tenths as shown.

Hundreds	Tens	Units	Tenths
		3	4

The rationale for this is that we move each digit to the right. So 3 tens becomes 3 units and 4 units becomes 4 tenths as shown above. The answer is written as 3.4. Similarly, when dividing by 100 or a 1000 the number is moved two and three places to the right as appropriate. We will now look at the technique below to work out the answer mechanically. This ensures you get the right answer without having to resort to the thousands, hundreds, tens, units, tenths and hundredths column. The simple rules shown below may help those students who find the above process difficult.

Chapter 2:   Arithmetic Part 2

Most questions in the numerical reasoning tests will require several steps and include various operations i.e. **+, - , x and ÷**

Time Based Questions

For converting time from 12 hour clock to 24 hour clock see examples below

12 –Hour Clock	24 –Hour Clock
8.45 am	08:45
11.30 am	11:30
12.20pm	12:20
2.35 pm	14: 35 (after 12pm add the appropriate minutes and hours to 12 hours, in this case 2hrs 35mins +12hrs = 14:35)
8.45 pm	20:45 (8hrs 45mins + 12hrs = 20:45)
11.47pm	23:47 (11hrs 47mins +12hrs = 23:47)

The Convention is that if the time is in 24-hr clock there is no need to put hrs after the time.

Also remember: 2.5 hours = 2 hours 30minutes (0.5 hours = half of 60 minutes)

2.25 hours = Two and a quarter hours = 2hrs 15 minutes

2.4 hours = 2 hours 24 minutes (0.4 hours = 0.4X60 = 24 minutes)

2.1 hours = 2 hours 6 minutes (0.1hours = 0.1 X 60 = 6 minutes)

For other time based questions e.g. years, months, days, hours, minutes or seconds remember the appropriate units.

Example 1: At a company new candidates are mentored once a week for 12 minutes each. There are 15 candidates who are being mentored. There is also a break for 20 minutes. The session starts at 11.30am. When does it finish? Give your answer using the 24 hour clock

Method: Clearly we need to first work out the total time it takes for all the candidates. Total time for 15 candidates is 15 X 12 = (15 X10 +15x2) =180 minutes = 3 hours plus break time of 20 minutes. So the mentoring session ends 3hrs and 20 minutes after 11.30am – this means it ends at 2.50pm. However using the 24 hour clock the times it ends is 14:50

Example 2: Peter completes a lap in 2.3 minutes. How many minutes and seconds is this?

Method: Convert 0.3 minutes into seconds. Since one whole minute = 60 seconds, then 0.3 minutes = 0.3X60 = 18 seconds. Hence Peter completes the lap in 2 minutes and 18 seconds.

(Note that 0.3 X 60 is the same as 3 X 6, hence this is equivalent to 18)

General Multiplication questions

Example 1: There are 4 medium size boxes containing 18 black jumpers each and 3 bigger boxes containing 23 black jumpers each. How many black jumpers are there altogether?

Method: 4 boxes of 18 each imply there are $4 \times 18 = 72$ black jumpers

(Another way of working out 4×18 is to break it down as follows: $4 \times 18 = 4 \times 10 + 4 \times 8 = 40 + 32 = 72$)

Similarly, 3 boxes of 23 each means, $3 \times 23 = 69$ black jumpers

Finally, $72 + 69 = 70 + 2 + 60 + 9 = 130 + 11 = 141$

There are a total of 141 black jumpers altogether

Example 2: I buy 5 books for £3.97 each. How much change do I get from a £20 note?

Method: Round up each book to £4. Hence the cost of 5 books $= £4 \times 5 - 5 \times 3p = £20 - 15p = £19.85$

You can see straight away that I get 15p change from my £20 note

More multiplication methods that may be helpful

The Grid Method of Multiplication

This is a very powerful method for those who find traditional long multiplication methods difficult.

Example 1: Multiply 37×6

Re-write the number 37 as 30 and 7 and re-write as shown in the grid table.

×	30	7
6	180	42

Now simply add up all the numbers inside the grid. So the answer is 180+42 =222

Example 2: work out 15×13

To work this out using the grid method, re-write 15 as 10 and 5, and 13 as 10 and 3 as shown on the outside of the grid table.

×	10	5
10	100	50
3	30	15

Multiply out the outside horizontal numbers with the outside vertical numbers to get the numbers inside as shown. Finally, just add up the inside numbers which in this case is 100+50+30+15 =195

Multiplication with decimals

Example 3: Work out 1.5×1.3

Step1: Leave out the decimal points and just work out the answer to 15×13 as shown above.

We know the answer to this is 195.

Step2: Now count the number of digits there are from the right before the decimal place for each number being multiplied and add them up. That is one for the first number and one for the second number to give a total of 2.

Step3: In the answer 195 count two from the right hand side and insert the decimal point.

So the answer is 1.95

Example 4: Work out 0.15×1.3

We know the answer to 15×13 is 195

This time the number of digits for each number before the decimal point is 2 for the first number and 1 for the second number giving a total of 3.

We now count 3 places from the right and insert a decimal point.

So the answer is 0.195

If you want to you can think of getting the answer another way:

Consider **Example 3** again: Multiply 1.5×1.3

We know the answer is 195. Note the fact that 1.5 is 15 divided by 10 and 1.3 is 13 divided by 10. So the answer is simply 195 divided by $10 \times 10 = 100$, so we divide 195 by 100 to get the answer as 1.95

More Multiplication

We will look at some fascinating ways of quickly multiplying by 11, 9, and 5, which will help you speed up your number work in mental arithmetic

Multiplying quickly by 11

One common method used is to multiply by 10 and then add the number itself. We will now look at a super- efficient method that is rarely used.

Super-efficient Speed Method:

11 × 11 =121 (the first and last digits remain the same & the middle number is the sum of the first two digits)

The basic method is: Start with the first digit, add the next two, until the last one. This method works with any number of digits.

Let us explore a few more examples with two digit numbers.

13 × 11= 143 (Keep the first and last digit of the number 13 the same, add 1 & 3 to give the middle number 4)

14 × 11= 154

19 × 11= 1(10)9=209 (Notice the middle number is 10, since 1+9=10, so we need to carry 1 to the left hand number)

A few more examples will show the power of this method.

27 × 11= 297 (the first number=2, the middle number=2+7, the last number =7)

28 × 11=2(10)8= 308 (using similar analysis to 19 X 11 above)

The same principle applies to numbers with more than 2 digits.

Example: Work out 215 × 11

Method: Keep the first and the last digit the same. Starting from the first digit add the subsequent digit to get the next digit, do this again with the second digit until the last digit which stays the same. So, 215 × 11 =2365 (2, is the first digit so stays the same, the sum of 2 and 1 gives you the next digit 3, the sum of 1 and 5 gives you the third digit 6 and finally the last digit 5 stays the same)

Example involving multiplying by 11

In a certain company 54 insurance agents manage to sell 11 insurance policies each in a particular month.

How many insurance policies did these agents sell altogether in that month?

54 × 11 using the method explained above is 594

Hence, total insurance policies sold in this month by these agents = 594 (Method: Keep the first and last digit of the number 54 he same, add 5 & 4 to give the middle number 9)

Multiplying quickly by 9

Here is an easy method to work out the 9× table

Example 1: Work out 9×7

Method

Step1: Add '0' to the number you are going to multiply by 9, e.g. 7 to get 70

Step2: Now subtract 7 from 70 to get 63 which is the final answer

Example 2: Work out 9 × 35

Method

Step1: Add '0' to the number you are going to multiply by 9, i.e. 35 to get 350

Step2: Now subtract 35 from 350 to get 315 which is the final answer

Example 3: Work out 9×78

Method

Step1: Add '0' to the number you are going to multiply by 9, e.g. 78 to get 780

Step2: Now subtract 78 from 780 to get 702 which is the final answer

A quick way of multiplying by 5

Multiply the number by 10 and halve the answer.

Example 1: $5 \times 4 =$ half of $10 \times 4 =$ half of $40 = 20$

Example 2: $5 \times 16 =$ half of $10 \times 16 =$ half of $160 = 80$

Example 3: $5 \times 23 =$ half of $10 \times 23 =$ half of $230 = 115$

TIP: Remember the Order of Arithmetical Operations

Remembering the order in which you do arithmetical operations is very important.

The rule taught traditionally is that of **BIDMAS.**

The **BIDMAS** rule is as follows:

(1) Always work out the **B**racket(s) first
(2) Then work out the **I**ndices of a number (squares, cubes, square roots and so on)
(3) Now **M**ultiply and **D**ivide
(4) Finally do the **A**ddition and **S**ubtraction.

Example 1: Work out $2 + 8 \times 3$

Do the multiplication before the addition

So $8 \times 3 = 24$ then add 2 to get 26

Example 2: $4 + 13(7 - 2)$ this means add 4 to $13 \times (7 - 2)$

Do the **brackets first** so $7 - 2 = 5$, **then multiply** 5 by 13 to get 65 and **finally add** 4 to get 69

Example 3: work out $3^2 \times 5 - 9$

(3^2 means 3×3 or 3 squared)

Work out the **square of 3 first**, then **multiply by 5** and finally **subtract 9** from the result.

So we have $3 \times 3 = 9$, $9 \times 5 = 45$ and finally $45 - 9 = 36$

Summary: When working out sums involving mixed operations (e.g. +, - , x and ÷) you need to work out the steps in stages using the BIDMAS rule: So to work out $8 + 25 \times 12$

Do the multiplication first, $25 \times 12 = 300$, write down 300 then add 8 to get the answer 308.

Division

In general the traditional short division approach is a good method. However, there are some other smart techniques worth considering for special situations.

Dividing a number by 2 is a very useful skill, since if you can divide by 2, you can by halving it again divide by 4 and halving it again divide by 8.

Dividing by 2, 4 and 8

Simply halve the number to divide by 2

(Some find it difficult to halve a number like 13. An alternative strategy is to multiply the number by 5 and divide by 10)

Halving again is the same as dividing by 4

And halving once more is the same as dividing by 8

Example 1: $28 \div 2 = 14$

Example 2: $268 \div 4 = 134 \div 2 = 67$

Example 3: $568 \div 8 = 284 \div 4 = 142 \div 2 = 71$

Example 4: $65 \div 4 = 32.5 \div 2 = 16.25$

Dividing by 5

An easy way to do this is to multiply the number by 2 and divide by 10.

Example 1: $\quad 120 \div 5 = (120 \times 2) \div 10 = 240 \div 10 = 24$

Example 2: $\quad 127 \div 5 = (127 \times 2) \div 10 = 254 \div 10 = 25.4$

Similarly to divide by 50 simply multiply by 2 and divide by 100

Dividing by 25

A good way to do this is to multiply by 4 and divide by 100.

Example 1: $240 \div 25 = (240 \times 4) \div 100 = 960 \div 100 = 9.6$

Example 2: $700 \div 25 = (700 \times 4) \div 100 = 2800 \div 100 = 28$

Dividing by other numbers: The conventional short division method is a good method but you might find the speed methods below useful sometimes.

Question involving division

Example: In one particular week, in a restaurant a bonus of £67.50 is divided amongst three waiters. How much does each one get in that week?

Clearly this is the same as $60 \div 3$ added to $7.5 \div 3$

$60 \div 3 = 20$ and $7.5 \div 3 = 2.5$ which altogether is 22.5

Hence, £67.5 $\div 3 = £22.50$ per waiter

Example 1: Divide 145 by 7

(145 = 140 +5)

We can say that $140 \div 7 = 20$, and then we are left with 5/7. So the answer is 20 and 5/7

Example 2: Divide 103 ÷ 9

$(103 = 99 + 4) = 99 \div 9 + 4/9 = 11$ and 4/9

Rounding numbers and estimating

We will start simply with rounding numbers to the nearest 10 and 100

Consider the number 271

Rounded to the nearest 10 this number is 270

Rounded to the nearest 100 this number is 300

(The principle is that if the right hand digit is lower than 5 you drop this number and replace it by 0. Conversely if the number is 5 or more drop that digit and add 1 to the left)

Try a few more:

5382 to the nearest 10 is 5380

5382 to the nearest hundred is 5400

5382 to the nearest 1000 is 5000

This rule can also be applied to decimal numbers:

3.7653 rounded to the nearest thousandth is 3.765

3.7653 rounded to the nearest hundredth is 3.77

3.7653 rounded to the nearest tenth is 3.8

3.7653 rounded to the nearest unit is 4

Tip: remember to use common sense when rounding in real life situations:

Example: A book store wants to keep 120 books in the same size boxes. They can fit 22 books in a box. How many boxes will they need?

Method: Number of boxes required will be 120÷22= 5.5 (to one decimal place). But clearly, they cannot have 5.5 boxes. So they need to have 6 boxes

---

Estimating calculations quickly

Example 1: Work out $(2.2 \times 7.12)/4.12$

We can quickly estimate that this is roughly equal to $(2 \times 7)/4 = 14/4$ which is around 3.5 or 4 rounded to the nearest unit. The actual answer is: 3.8 (to 1 decimal place)

Example 2: Work out $38 \times 2.9 \times 0.53$

We can approximate 38 to be 40 to the nearest ten, we can approximate 2.9 o 3 to the nearest unit. We can approximate 0.53 to 0.5 to the nearest tenth. So the magnitude of the answer is $40 \times 3 \times 0.5$. This is $120 \times 0.5 = 60$ (approximately)

Now consider Significant Figures (s.f.)

Normally, the first digit is the first significant figure except when it is 0, when you do not count it. Remember to get the size of the number right when working out significant figures.

Example 1: Write 53.6 to 1 s.f. The answer is 50 (It is not 5)

Example 2: Write 262.7 to 2 s.f. The answer is 260 (It is not 26)

Example 3: Write 0.0384 to 1 s.f. The answer is 0.04 (ignore the 0 at the beginning)

Chapter 3: Arithmetic Part 3

Fractions, decimals and percentages

I am sure most of you are aware that $\frac{1}{2}$ =0.5. This in turn is equal to 50%.

It is worth reviewing this fact. In addition, you should try and remember the following other equivalences if you have forgotten them:

Fractions, decimals and percentage equivalents

Fractions	Decimal	Percentage
$\frac{1}{2}$	0.5	50%
$\frac{1}{4}$	0.25	25%
$\frac{3}{4}$	0.75	75%
$\frac{1}{10}$	0.1	10%
$\frac{1}{5}$	0.2	20%

If, we know $\dfrac{1}{2}$ = 0.5

We can deduce that $\dfrac{1}{4}$ = 0.25

(Since a quarter is half of half)

Similarly $\dfrac{1}{8}$ is 0.125

We can do this quickly because all we do is halve each decimal value.

Half of 0.5 is 0.25, Half of 0.25 is 0.125

We can of course continue this process.

Further if we know $\dfrac{1}{10}$ =0.1 we can now work out $\dfrac{2}{10}, \dfrac{3}{10}, \dfrac{7}{10}$ etc.

$\dfrac{2}{10}$ = 0.2 (2 × 0.1), $\dfrac{3}{10}$ = 0.3 (3 × 0.1, $\dfrac{7}{10}$ = 0.7 (7 × 0.1), $\dfrac{9}{10}$ = 0.9 (9 × 0.1)

Another useful fraction and decimal equivalent to remember is $\dfrac{1}{3}$ =0.333… (0.3 recurring)

The key equivalent percentages to remember are as follows:

$\dfrac{3}{4}$ = 75%, $\dfrac{1}{2}$ =50%, $\dfrac{1}{4}$ = 25%, $\dfrac{1}{8}$ = 12.5%, $\dfrac{1}{10}$ = 10%

See summary box below

Summary:

Remember the following equivalences

$\frac{1}{2}$ =0.5 =50%, $\frac{1}{4}$ =0.25 =25%, $\frac{3}{4}$ =0.75 =75%, $\frac{1}{10}$ =0.1=10%

Also if you can try to remember, $\frac{1}{5}$ =0 .2 = 20%, and $\frac{2}{5}$ =0.4 =40%, $\frac{1}{3}$ =0.333... (0.3 recurring) = 33.33% (to 2 decimal places)

To convert a fraction into a percentage, simply multiply the fraction by 100

Questions involving percentages and fractions

Example 1: Find 25% of £250

Method: Find 50% of £250 and halve it again.

Half of £250 = £125, Half of £125 =£62.50, so 25% of £250 = £62.50

Example 2: In a marketing department of 25 people there are 12 women and the rest are men.

(1) What fraction of the marketing department consists of men?

(2) What percentage is this?

(1) Since there are 12 women, there are 13 men out of 25. So the fraction of men is $\frac{13}{25}$

(2) The percentage of men is $\frac{13}{25}$ × 100 = 52%, (Divide 100 by 25 to get 4. Then multiply 13 by 4 to get 52%)

Example 3: 30% of the applicants for a certain job are male. There are 30 candidates in total. How many of the applicants are female?

Method: If 30% of the applicants are male, this means 70% are female. So we need to find 70% of 30 candidates. Since 10% of 30 is 3, this means 70% corresponds to 3X7 = 21 females. Hence, 21 of the candidates are female.

Working out increase or decrease in percentages from original value

Example 1: In a certain corner shop 16 packs of cereal A were sold in week 1. In the same shop 20 packs of the same cereal were sold in week 2. What was the percentage increase in the cereal packs A sold from week 1 to week 2?

Method: Increase in number of cereal packs A = 20 – 16 =4. Original number of cereal packs =16. The increase of 4 was based on 16 cereal packs. To work out the percentage increase we simply divide the increase by the original number of cereal packs and multiply this by 100. That is $\frac{4}{16} \times 100 = \frac{1}{4} \times 100 = 25\%$

To work out decrease in percentages (uses the same principle as above)

Example 2: The original price of a projector was: £150, the new price is reduced to £135. What is the percentage decrease in price? The decrease in price is £150 - £135 = £15. The decrease over the original price is $\frac{15}{150}$. To turn this into a percentage we multiply $\frac{15}{150} \times 100 = \frac{1500}{150} = 10\%$. So the decrease in percentage price is 10%.

The basic formula to work out increase or decrease percentage change is shown below:

$$\frac{difference\ between\ final\ and\ original\ value}{original\ value} \times 100$$

One thing to remember though is that the increase or decrease in percentage points is different from increase or decrease in percentages.

To illustrate this consider the example below:

The unemployment rate in a region A was 8% in 2010. In 2011 the unemployment rate in the same region was 10%. **(1)** What was the **percentage point** increase in unemployment from 2010 to 2011? **(2)** What is the **percentage increase** in unemployment from 2010 to 2011?

(1) The **percentage point** increase is simply 2% (i.e. from 8% to 10%)

(2) However the **percentage increase** in unemployment is $\frac{2}{8} \times 100 = \frac{200}{8} = \frac{100}{4} = 25\%$.

In the Numerical reasoning test context, if you are asked to work out the **percentage point increase,** say in sales in Product A changing from 20% to 30%. The answer is obviously 10%. But if asked to work out the **percentage increase,** then the answer is $\frac{10}{20} \times 100 = \frac{1000}{20} = \frac{100}{2} = 50\%$

Miscellaneous questions involving fractions and percentages

Example 1: Finding fraction of an amount

Find $\frac{3}{4}$ of £600, First find $\frac{1}{2}$ = £300, then find $\frac{1}{4}$ (which is half of half) = £150

Therefore $\frac{3}{4}$ = £450 (adding half plus a quarter)

Example 2: Finding a fraction and turning it into a percentage

There are 40 builders in a small town in Yorkshire. In a particular month 5 builders are without work.

What is the percentage of builders that do not have work in this month in this small town?

The fraction of builders without work = $\frac{5}{40}$, by dividing top and bottom numbers

by 5 we get $\frac{1}{8}$.

To convert 1/8 into a percentage simply multiply 1/8 by 100

= 1/8 x100 =100/8 = 50/4 =25/2 =12.5%

(Another method: We know ¼ =25%

Hence 1/8 =12.5% (Since 1/8 is half of a quarter)

Calculator based questions

You need to remember that percent means out of 100. That is $\frac{1}{100}$. So to find say 42.5% of a number, divide the number by 100 and multiply it by 42.5.

Example: work out 42.5% of £400

We can say that this is the same as (£400 ÷ 100) × 42.5 =4 × 42.5 = £170

Try working this out with a basic calculator to see if you agree with the answer.

Do the calculations in steps. For example to work out 3.65 + 15X6

Use the rule that you always do multiplication and division before you do addition and subtraction. So to work out 3.65 +15×6, we work out 15×6 first. This gives us 90, then we add 3.65 to 90 to give us 93.65 as the final answer. Note to clear the answer simply click on [C] on the calculator.

Simple Interest and Compound Interest

Simple Interest

Example 1: I have £5000 in a building society account which pays me simple interest of 3% per annum. I keep my money for 3 years. How much in total will I have at the end of the 3 year period?

Method: At the end of the first year the total interest I will receive is 3% of £5000.

This is $\dfrac{3}{100} X 5000 = \dfrac{15000}{100} = £150$ per annum.

At the end of 3 years I will receive 3×£150 = £450 total interest. This means the total amount I will have is £5450 (original £5000 plus 3 years of simple interest)

You can if you like use the formula below to work out the total simple interest over a given period of time.

I =PRT , where I = Total interest, P = Principal amount (original amount), R is the annual interest rate and T = the time in years.

So in the above case I =5000× $\dfrac{3}{100} X 3 = £5000 \times \dfrac{9}{100} = £450$

Finally, to find the total amount we have at the end of the 3 year period, we simply add £450 to the original £5000 to get £5450

Example 2: Work out the final amount at the end of one year if there is a 10% increase per annum and I have $3000 to start with.

The traditional method is to work out 10% of $3000 first. Then add this answer to $3000 to get the final answer. 10% of $3000 = $300. So the final price after a 10% increase is $3000 + $300 =$3300

Here is fast and efficient method to work out the final answer.

Simply work out 1.1X5000

Since 1.1 denotes a 10% increase.

Why 1.1? Since 100% plus 10% =1 + 0.1 = 1.1

Now 1.1× 3000 = $3300 which is the final answer

Compound Interest

Now consider a problem involving recurring percentage changes

Example 1:

Find the value of $5000 if I gain a profit of 10% the first year followed by (10% of the new amount) in the second year. (This is called compound interest)

THIS MEANS THE INCREASE IS 1.1X FOLLOWED BY 1.1X AGAIN

Or $(1.1)^2 \times 5000$

$(1.1)^2 \times 5000 = 1.21 \times 5000 = \$6050$

So the final value is $6050

Example 2:

I buy a one bedroom apartment for $200,000. It increases in value by 5% per annum

How much will it be worth in 15 years?

Method: Increase after 1 year will be 1.05×$200,000, after two years it will be: $(1.05)^2 \times \$200,000$, after three years it will be $(1.05)^3 \times \$200,000$. So, after 15 years it will be worth $(1.05)^{15} \times \$200,000 = \$415786$

Example 3:

A car depreciates by 30% per annum. I buy it at £18000. What is its value in 5 years' time? Give your answer to the nearest pound

Method:

After one year its value will decrease by 30%, so its new value will be 70% of original as shown below:

£18000×0.7, hence, after five years its value will be $18000×(0.7)^5

Value after five years is £3025

Example 4:

I have a house that is currently valued at £300,000. House prices are predicted to fall 7% per annum for the next two years followed by a 5% growth for a subsequent five years. What is the value of my house after seven years?

Method:

The value of my house changes by 'depreciating' for two years followed by 'appreciating' for the subsequent five years.

So the value is £300000×$(0.93)^2$ × $(1.05)^5$

= £331157 (to the nearest pound)

(Note: 0.93 denotes the depreciation by 7%, and 1.05 denotes the growth by 5%)

Chapter 4:   Arithmetic Part 4   Fractions

Simplifying fractions

Reducing a fraction to its lowest terms

Basically you need to find numbers that divide into the top number (numerator) as well as the bottom number (denominator), and then divide them both by the same number (start with 2, if doesn't go then choose 3, then 5, and then the next prime factor e.g. 7, 11, etc.)

Example 1: Reduce $\frac{16}{24}$ to its lowest terms.

8 divides exactly into 16 and 24, so in the fraction $\frac{16}{24}$ divide top and bottom by 8. This gives the answer as $\frac{2}{3}$

In case you can't see this straight away, try starting with the number two and work your way numerically upwards using the next prime factor i.e. try 3, then 5 etc. if required

So for the fraction $\frac{16}{24}$ we can start dividing top and bottom by 2 to give us $\frac{8}{12}$,

then do the same again as both 8 and 12 are still divisible by 2. This gives us $\frac{4}{6}$ and

finally repeating the process once more reduces the fraction to $\frac{2}{3}$ which is the

simplest form.

Example 2:

Simplify $\frac{9}{12}$ to its lowest terms

In this case we can't divide top and bottom by 2, so we try 3. Since 3 will go into both 9 and 12, we can reduce this to the fraction $\frac{3}{4}$ (since 9 ÷3 =3 and 12 ÷ 3 =4)

Hence, $\frac{9}{12}$ reduces to $\frac{3}{4}$

Example 3:

Reduce fraction $\frac{49}{77}$ to its lowest terms. This time we need to spot that 2, 3, 5, does not go into either 49, or 77. Either by trial and error or by spotting the right number we notice 7 goes into both the numerator and the denominator. This reduces

$\frac{49}{77}$ to $\frac{7}{11}$

Cancelling down a fraction to its simplest form (lowest term)

To simplify a fraction to its lowest terms you divide the numerator and the denominator by the same prime factors (2, 3, 5, 7, 11, etc.) to give the equivalent fractions as shown in the examples above

---

Finding fraction of an amount

Example 1: Find $\frac{2}{5}$ of 25, simply replace the 'of' by ×. (times)

So $\frac{2}{5}$ of 25 becomes $\frac{2}{5}$ × 25

To work this out find out 1/5 of 25 and then multiply the answer by 2. So 25 divided by 5, equals 5, then 2 × 5 =10. Hence $\frac{2}{5}$ of 25 =10

Example:

60 people apply for a certain job vacancy. 12 people are short-listed for an interview. What is the proportion of people that are not short listed for the interview? Give your answer as a decimal.

Total number of people applying for this job = 60, Since 12 people are shortlisted, this means 48 are not shortlisted. Hence the proportion that is not shortlisted = 48/60. If you divide top and bottom by 6, this simplifies to 8/10.

The answer as a decimal is 0.8

Adding and Subtracting Fractions

This next section will help you revise adding, subtracting, multiplying and dividing fractions together

Consider adding and subtracting fractions together.

When the bottom numbers (denominators) are the same, just add the top numbers together keeping the bottom number the same, likewise for subtraction just subtract the top two numbers.

Example 1: $\dfrac{2}{5} + \dfrac{1}{5} = \dfrac{3}{5}$

Example 2: $\dfrac{2}{5} - \dfrac{1}{5} = \dfrac{1}{5}$

When the denominators are different

Example 3: Work out $\dfrac{1}{2} + \dfrac{2}{5}$

When the denominators are different, the traditional method of doing this is to find the lowest common denominator. We have to find a number that both 2 and 5 will go into. This is clearly 10.

We can now re-write the fraction with the same common denominator.

To do this we have to ask how did we get the denominator from 2 to 10 for the first part, and likewise for the second part from 5 to 10. The answer is shown below:

$$\frac{1 X 5}{2 X 5} + \frac{2 X 2}{5 X 2} = \frac{5}{10} + \frac{4}{10} = \frac{9}{10}$$

We had to multiply top and bottom by 5 for the first part and top and bottom by 2 for the second part as shown above. We can then add the fraction as we have the same common denominator.

We can however use another very simple strategy that always works. The method is that of crosswise multiplication.

The basic method is to take the fraction sum and do crosswise multiplication as shown by the arrows. In addition, multiply the denominators (bottom numbers) together to get the new denominator.

Example 1: $\dfrac{1}{2} + \dfrac{2}{5} = \dfrac{1}{2} \diagup\!\!\!\!\diagdown \dfrac{2}{5} = \dfrac{1X5+2X2}{2X5} = \dfrac{5+4}{10} = \dfrac{9}{10}$

We notice that if we cross multiply as shown we get 1 X 5 and 2 X 2 respectively at the top. To get the bottom number we simply multiply the bottom numbers, 2 and 5 together. So the denominator is 2 X 5=10.

Let us try another example:

Example 2: Work out $\dfrac{3}{7} + \dfrac{2}{5}$

Using crosswise multiplication and adding rule, as well as multiplying the bottom two numbers we get:

$$\dfrac{3}{7} \diagup\!\!\!\!\diagdown \dfrac{2}{5} = \dfrac{3X5+7X2}{35} = \dfrac{15+14}{35} = \dfrac{29}{35}$$

This is a very elegant method which always works

Example 3: Work out $\dfrac{3}{7} - \dfrac{2}{5}$

This is similar to the above except instead of adding we now subtract as shown below.

$$\dfrac{3}{7} \diagup\!\!\!\!\diagdown \dfrac{2}{5} = \dfrac{3X5-7X2}{35} = \dfrac{15-14}{35} = \dfrac{1}{35}$$

Note: In fact you can use this method when adding or subtracting any fraction that you find difficult. Even if you use this method for simple cases, you will still get the right answer but you may have to cancel down to get the lowest terms for the final answer.

For example we know that $\dfrac{1}{4} + \dfrac{1}{2} = \dfrac{3}{4}$

But if we didn't know and used the method shown we would get $\dfrac{1}{4} \diagdown\!\!\!\!\diagup \dfrac{1}{2} =$

$\dfrac{1X2+4X1}{4X2} = \dfrac{2+4}{8} = \dfrac{6}{8} = \dfrac{3}{4}$ (we get this by dividing both the numerator and denominator in $\dfrac{6}{8}$ by 2). So we get the same answer in the end

Question involving fractions

(1) Find $2\dfrac{3}{4}$ of £64

We first work out 2 X 64 = 128, to work out three quarters of 64 we first work out a half and then add it to a quarter of 64.

Half of £64 is £32

A quarter of £64 (is half of £32) is £16

Hence three quarters of £64 = £32 + £16 = £48

So two and three quarters of £64 = £128 + £48 = £176

Adding and subtracting mixed numbers

We first add or subtract the whole numbers and then the fractional parts.

Example 1: $2\dfrac{2}{5} + 4\dfrac{3}{7}$

Adding the whole numbers we get 6. (Simply add 2 and 4)

Now add the fractional parts to get: $\dfrac{14+15}{35} = \dfrac{29}{35}$

So the answer is $6\dfrac{29}{35}$

Example 2: $4\dfrac{3}{7} - 2\dfrac{2}{5}$

Subtract the whole numbers and then the fractional parts, which gives us:

$$2\dfrac{15-14}{35} = 2\dfrac{1}{35}$$

Multiplying Fractions

Multiplying fractions by the traditional method is quite efficient so we will consider only this approach.

Example 1: $\dfrac{2}{3} \times \dfrac{5}{7} = \dfrac{10}{21}$

In this case we simply multiply the top two numbers to get the new numerator and multiply the bottom two numbers together to get the new denominator, as shown above.

Another example will help consolidate this process:

Example 2: $\dfrac{10}{21} \times \dfrac{5}{7} = \dfrac{50}{147}$

(Multiply 10×5 to get 50 for the numerator and 21×7 to get 147 for the denominator)

Division of Fractions

When dividing fractions we invert the second fraction and multiply as shown.

Think of an obvious example. If we have to divide ½ by ¼ we intuitively know that the answer is 2. The reason for this is that there are 2 quarters in one half. Let us see how this works in practice.

Example 1: $\dfrac{1}{2} \div \dfrac{1}{4} = \dfrac{1}{2} X \dfrac{4}{1} = \dfrac{4}{2} = 2$

Step 1: Re-write fraction as a multiplication sum with the second fraction inverted.

Step 2: Work out the fraction as a normal multiplication

Step 3: Simplify if possible. In this case 4 divided by 2 is 2.

Example 2: $\dfrac{6}{11} \div \dfrac{5}{11} = \dfrac{6}{11} X \dfrac{11}{5} = \dfrac{66}{55} = \dfrac{6}{5} = 1\dfrac{1}{5}$

Step1: Re-write the fraction inverting the second fraction as shown

Step2: Multiply the top part and the bottom part to get $\dfrac{66}{55}$ **as shown.**

Step 3: Simplify this by dividing top and bottom by 11 to get $\dfrac{6}{5}$ **. Now this finally simplifies to** $1\dfrac{1}{5}$ **as shown.**

The following steps are required to convert a mixed number into a fraction. Consider the mixed fraction $2\frac{1}{4}$.

Step 1: Multiply the denominator of the fractional part by the whole number and add the numerator. In this case this works out to $2 \times 4 + 1 = 9$. This now becomes the new numerator.

Step 2: The denominator stays the same as before. Now re-write the new fraction as $\frac{9}{4}$. (That is the new numerator ÷ existing denominator)

Let us look at another example. Convert the mixed number, $3\frac{3}{7}$ into a fraction.

Step 1: Multiply denominator of fractional part by whole number and add the numerator. This gives $3 \times 7 + 3 = 24$ as the new numerator.

Step2: Re-write fraction as new fraction. This is now the new numerator ÷ existing denominator. This gives us $\frac{24}{7}$

Multiplying mixed numbers together

Consider the examples below:

Example: $1\frac{1}{5} \ X \ 1\frac{3}{8}$

The method is simply to convert both mixed numbers into fractions and multiply as shown below:

$$1\frac{1}{5} x 1\frac{3}{8} = \frac{6}{5} x \frac{11}{8} = \frac{66}{40} = 1\frac{26}{40} = 1\frac{13}{20}$$

(Notice $\frac{26}{40}$ simplifies to $\frac{13}{20}$)

Dividing mixed numbers together

Example: $1\dfrac{1}{2} \div 1\dfrac{1}{4}$

There are two steps required to work out the division of mixed numbers.

Step1: Convert both mixed numbers into fractions as before

Step 2: Multiply the fractions together but invert the second one.

$$1\dfrac{1}{2} \div 1\dfrac{1}{4} = \dfrac{3}{2} \div \dfrac{5}{4} = \dfrac{3}{2} \text{ x } \dfrac{4}{5} = \dfrac{12}{10} = 1\dfrac{2}{10} = 1\dfrac{1}{5}$$

Chapter 5:   Proportions and ratios

Although proportion and ratio are related they are not the same thing – see example below for clarification.

Example: In a class there are 15 girls and 10 boys. The **ratio of girls to boys is** 15:10, or 3:2, (divide both 15 and 10 by 5) and the **proportion of girls in the class** is 15 out of 25, $\dfrac{15}{25}$ **which simplifies to** $\dfrac{3}{5}$

Questions based on proportions and ratios

Example 1:

In a class of 27 pupils, 9 go home for lunch. What is the proportion of pupils in this class that have lunch at school?

Since 9 out of 27 pupils go home, this means 18 pupils have lunch at school.

As a proportion this is 18 out of 27 or $\dfrac{18}{27}$ which simplifies to $\dfrac{2}{3}$

Example 2: In a certain work place the ratio of males to females is 2: 3. There are 250 workers altogether. How many of these are male?

Step 1: Find out the total number of parts. You can do this by adding up the ratio parts together. E.g. 2:3 means there are (2+3) = 5 parts altogether. This means 1 part = one fifth of 250 workers = 50 workers.

Step 2: Since the ratio of male to female is 2:3, there are 2×50 males and 3×50 females

The number of males in this workplace =2×50 = 100

Example 3:

$100 is divided in the ratio 1: 4 how much is the bigger part?

The total number of parts that $100 is divided into is 5 (to find the number of parts simply add the numbers in the ratio, which in this case is 1 and 4)

Clearly, 1 part equals $20 (100 divided by 5), so 4 parts is equal to $80. This is the required bigger part.

Example 4:

$1500 is divided in the ratio of 3 :5 :7

Find out how much the smallest part is worth?

Clearly $1500 is divided into a total of 15 Parts

So each part is worth $100 ($1500 divided by 15)

So 3 parts (this is the smallest part) equals $300

Example 5:

Two lengths are in the ratio 3: 5. If the first length is 150m what is the second length?

If the ratio is 3: 5 then the lengths are in the ratio 150: n (where n is the second length)

We now need to determine n. We can see that 150 is 50 times 3.

So, n (which is the second length) must be 50 times 5, which equals 250m.

Example 6:

As we have seen, sometimes ratios are expressed in ways, which may not be the simplest form. Consider 5 : 10

(a) You can re-write 5 : 10 as 1 : 2 (divide both sides by 5)

(b) 4 : 10 can be re-written as 2 : 5

(c) 8 : 60 can be re-written as 4 : 30 which simplifies to 2 : 15

(d) 15 : 36 simplifies to 5 : 12 (divide both sides by 3)

Example 7: The width and the length of the room are in the ratio 2: 3.

What is the length of the room if the width is 4.5m?

This means the ratio of width to length is w : 1 = 2 : 3. We can re-write this as

4.5 : 1 = 2 : 3. (If we now divide 4.5 by 2, we get 2.25), so the length = 2.25 × 3

= 6.75m.

Increasing & decreasing ratios

Example 1: A small building took 10 people 8 days to build. How long would it take 4 people to build?

Method: Time taken for 10 people = 8 days

So, time taken by 1 person would be 80 days

Hence, time taken by 4 people = 80÷4 = 20 days

Example 2: A recipe for a dessert for 4 people needs $\dfrac{3}{4}$ tablespoons of sugar. How many tablespoons of sugar do you need for 14 people?

Method: One person needs 3/4 ÷4 tablespoons of sugar = $\dfrac{3}{4} X \dfrac{1}{4} = \dfrac{3}{16}$

So the amount of sugar needed for 14 people = $\dfrac{3}{16} X \dfrac{14}{1} = \dfrac{42}{16} = \dfrac{21}{8} = 2\dfrac{5}{8}$

tablespoons or **just over two and half tablespoons** full of sugar

Example 3: A team of 10 people can deliver 6000 leaflets in a residential estate in 4 hours. How long does it take 6 people to deliver these leaflets?

Method: 1 person will take 10 times as long or 4×10 = 40hours

This means 6 people will take $40 \div 6 = 20 \div 3 = 6\frac{2}{3}$ hours = 6 hours and 40 minutes.

(Since 1/3 of an hour = 20 minutes)

Scales and ratios

Consider that you are reading a map and the scale ratio is 1: 100000

(This means for every one cm on the map the actual distance is 100000 cm or, put another way every one cm on the map, the distance = 1000 m (divide 100000 by 100 to get the result in metres. Now, 1000 m = 1km (divide 1000 by 1000 to get 1 since 1km =1000m)

(Scales can also be used in other areas such as architectural drawings)

Question based on scales

I note that the map I am using has a scale of 1: 25000. The distance between the two places I am interested in is 12cm. What is the actual distance in km?

Method: 12 cm on the map corresponds to 12 x 25000 = 300x 1000 =300000cm

=3000m = 3km. (300000 /100 to convert to metres = 3000 m, now divide 3000 by 1000 to convert to km). Hence the distance between the two places is 3km

---

Conversions

Conversions are often useful in changing currencies for example from pounds to dollars or euros and vice-versa. It is also useful to convert distances from miles to kilometers or weights from kilograms to pounds and so on.

Basically a conversion involves changing information from one unit of measurement to another. Consider some examples below:

Question based on conversions

Example 1:

I go to France with £150 and convert this into Euros at 1.2 Euros to a pound.

(1) How many Euros do I get? **(2)** I am left with 39 Euros when I get back home. The exchange rate remains the same. How many pounds do I get back?

Method: (1) Since 1 pound = 1.2 Euros, I get 150 × 1.2 =180 Euros in total.

(2) When I get back I change 39 Euros back into pounds. This time I need to divide 39 by 1.2

So 39÷1.2 =32.5. This means I get back £32.50

Example 2:

The formula for changing kilometers to miles is given by:

$M = \dfrac{5}{8} \times K$. Use this formula to convert 68 kilometers to miles

Method: substitute **K** with 68 and multiply by $\dfrac{5}{8}$

This means $M = \dfrac{5}{8} \times 68$. Using a calculator this comes to 42.5 miles

It is worth reviewing some common Metric and Imperial Measures as shown below

Metric Measures

1000 Millilitres (ml) =1 Litre(l)

100 Centilitres (cl) =1 Litre (l)

10ml =1 cl

1 Centimetre (cm) =10 Millimetres (mm)

1 Metre (m) = 100 cm

1 Kilometre (km) =1000 m

1 Kilogram (kg) =1000 grams (g)

Imperial Measurements

1 foot =12 inches

1 yard =3 feet

1 pound = 16 ounces

1 stone =14 pounds (lb)

1 gallon = 8 pints

1 inch = 2.54 cm (approximately)

Question on conversions

A ramblers' group goes on a walking tour whilst in the South of France. They walk from Perpignan to Canet Plage which is approximately 11 km away. After a lunch break and some time on the beach, they walk back to Perpignan. How many miles in total do they walk on that day? (You are given that 8 km is approximately equal to 5 miles.) Give your answer as a decimal.

Method: Total distance walked = 22Km (11 + 11). To convert this into miles we have to multiply 22 by 5 and then divide by 8 (Since 8 km = 5 miles)

That is $22 \times \dfrac{5}{8}$ =13.75 miles (simply multiply 22 by 5 and divide the answer by 8)

(Remember, use of calculator would be allowed for this type of question)

Chapter 6: Weighted Averages & Formulas

When two or more sets of data are combined together and some are more important than others, then different weightings are given. The weighted mean is then worked out appropriately as shown in the examples below:

Example 1:

In a particular subject the coursework carries a weight of 0.3 and the exam mark carries a weight of 0.7

Calculate the overall percentage result if a pupil got 60% for the coursework and 50% for the exam.

The percentage result is 60X0.3 + 50X0.7 = 18 +35 = 53%

Example 2

A pupil achieved the following marks in three tests

Test 1: 55 marks

Test 2: 60 marks

Test 3: 12 marks

The formula used by the head of maths to work the weighted average for all three tests combined was:

Overall weighted average = $\frac{Test1 \times 60}{100}$ + $\frac{Test2 \times 20}{60}$ + Test3

Using this formula we can work out the overall weighted score as:

$\frac{55 \times 60}{100}$ + $\frac{60 \times 20}{60}$ + 12

This works out to 33 + 20 +12 = 65 marks

Formula

A formula describes the relationship between two or more variables. Consider a simple case first.

Example 1: A company pays 40p per mile and certain meal expenses when their sales employees visit clients. The cost of claiming mileage is calculated using the formula given, payable at 40p per mile and a fixed cost of £25. The formula is C = M× 0.4 + 25, where C represents the cost in pounds payable to the employee by the company.

So for example if an employee has to travel 40 miles from her home to the client, the employee can claim 80 miles altogether for the journey to the client and back + £25 as shown below by the formula.

Using the formula we have C = 0.4×80 + 25 = 32 + 25 = £57

(Explanation of working out: Using BIDMAS we multiply before adding. So 0.4×80 =32, finally add 32 and 25 together to get 57)

Example 2:

(1) The formula for working out the distance depends on the speed and time taken in the appropriate units.

D = S×T where D is the distance, S the speed and T is the time.

What is the distance travelled if my speed is 60kmh and I travel for 1hour and 30 minutes.

1 hour 30 minutes corresponds to 1.5 hours so, using the formula, D = 60×1.5 = 90 km. That is, the distance equals 90km

(2) The formula for working out the speed is given as Speed= Distance/Time

That is S = D÷T

Work out the average speed with which I travel, if I cover 100 miles in 2.5 hours.

Since S = D÷T, this means S = 100÷2.5 =40 mph (Notice the units for the first example were in kilometres and units for the second example were in miles

---

(3) The formula for working out time taken is given by T = D÷S

Calculate the time taken to cover 90 miles if I travel at 60mph?

Time taken, T= D÷S, so T = 90÷60 = 9÷6 =3÷ 2 = 1.5 hours or 1 hour and 30 minutes.

Example 3:

The formula for converting the temperature from Celsius to Fahrenheit is given by the formula: $F= \dfrac{9}{5} C +32$ (where C is the temperature in degrees Centigrade)

If the temperature is 10 degrees Celsius then what is the equivalent temperature in Fahrenheit?

Using the formula $F= \dfrac{9}{5} C +32$, and substituting 10 in place of C, we have $F= \dfrac{9}{5} \times$ $10 +32 = \dfrac{90}{5} + 32 =18+32 =50$. Hence, 10 degrees centigrade = 50 degrees Fahrenheit

Explanation of working out above: Remember we multiply and divide before adding and subtracting. There are no brackets to worry about. When working out $\dfrac{9}{5}$ × 10 +32, multiply 9 by 10 to get 90, divide this by 5 to get 18, finally add 18 and 32 together to get 50

Example 4:   Convert 68 degrees Fahrenheit to degrees Celsius. The formula for converting the temperature from Fahrenheit to Celsius is given by: $C= \dfrac{5}{9}(F\text{-}32)$. To change 68 degrees Fahrenheit to degrees Celsius we can substitute for F in the formula $C= \dfrac{5}{9}(F - 32)$, C = $C= \dfrac{5}{9}(68 - 32)$. =5 × 36/9 = 5 × 4 =20

Hence, 68 degrees Fahrenheit =20 degrees Celsius

Explanation of the working out above: Using BIDMAS we work out the bracket first. This gives us 68-32 =36. We now divide this by 9 and multiply by 5. Clearly 36÷9 =4 and finally 5×4 =20)

We have seen that formulas can be important in conversion problems

Earlier we saw the formula: $S = D \div T$, that is, $\text{Speed} = \dfrac{\text{Distance}}{\text{Time}}$.

Sometimes in the On screen questions you may be shown a distance time graph for a school coach trip and asked to work out average speed for a particular part of the journey and the time the coach was stationary. See example below.

Example: A school trip by coach to a heritage site leaves at 1200hrs from the school. The coach arrives at the destination at 1300hrs. It then stops so the pupils can look around the site. Finally after looking around the site it leaves and arrives back at school at 15:30hrs. (1) How long did the coach stop for? (2) What was the average speed on the return journey?

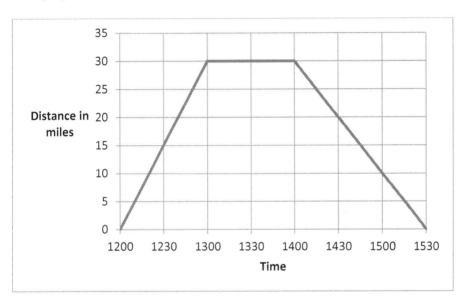

(1) From the distance-time graph above you can see it was stationary from 1300 – 1400hrs, which is 1hr

(Between these time intervals no further distance is covered, so it is stationary – see the vertical axis at 30 miles)

(2) The return journey starts at 1400hrs and ends at school at 1530hrs = 1.5 hrs.

Since $\textbf{\textit{Speed}} = \dfrac{\textit{Distance}}{\textit{Time}}$, this means speed = 30÷1.5 = 20 mph

You might find the following conversions useful to go through

(Typically the Numerical reasoning test questions give you the conversion formula in the relevant questions)

1 km = 5/8 mile

1 mile =8/5 km

1kg =2.2 lb (approximately)

1 gallon =4.5 litres (approximately)

1 inch = 2.54 cm (approximately)

Chapter 7: Number Sequences

Many numerical aptitude tests contain questions involving identifying number patterns in order to find the subsequent missing number(s).

Try these questions yourself and see how many you can do. Then check the answers and their rationale.

Complete the following sequences by finding the missing numbers:

(1) 4, 7, 10, 13, __ , __
(2) 21, 17, 13, 9, 5, __ , __
(3) 18, 9, 4.5, __ , __
(4) 0, 1, 1, 2, 3, 5, 8, __ , __
(5) 1, 4, 9, 16, 25, __, __
(6) 1, 8, 27, 64, __ , __
(7) 17, 12, 7, 2, __ , __
(8) 1, 6, 36, 216, __ , __
(9) 128, 32, 8, __ , __
(10) 36, 49, 64, 81, __ , __
(11) 11, 121, 1331, __ , __
(12) 0.142857, 0.285714, 0.428571, ____ , ____
(13) 81, 729, 6561, ____ , ____
(14) 1, 3, 6, 10, ____ , ____

Answers and their rationale:

(1) 16, 19 (each number increases by a constant value of 3)
(2) 1, -3 (each number decreases by a constant value of 4)
(3) 2.25, 1.125 (each number is half the previous number)
(4) 13, 21 (each number is the sum of the previous two numbers)
(5) 36, 49 (each number is the square of natural numbers, the first number is 1 × 1, the second number is 2 × 2, the third number is 3 × 3, ...the sixth number is 6 × 6, the seventh number is 7 × 7)
(6) 125, 216 (cubes of natural numbers. The first number is 1 × 1 × 1, the second number is 2 × 2 × 2, 3 × 3 × 3, ...5 × 5 × 5, 6 × 6 × 6)
(7) −3, -8 (numbers are decreasing by 5)
(8) 1296, 7776 (each number is 6× the previous number)
(9) 2, 1/2 (each number is a quarter of the previous number)
(10) 100, 121 (square numbers again, the previous number was 9 × 9, then 10 × 10 and finally 11 ×11)
(11) 14641, 161051 (each number is 11× the previous number)

61

(12) 0.571428, 0.714285 (these numbers are cyclic numbers each preceding starting number being the lower in the series, first number is $\frac{1}{7}$ as a decimal, second number is $\frac{2}{7}$ as a decimal, third number is $\frac{3}{7}$ as a decimal etc until we reach $\frac{7}{7}$ and then the cycle repeats itself – alternative explanation, the second number is twice the first number, the third number is three times the first number, the 4th number is four times the first number, etc)

(13) 59049, 531441 (each number is 9× the previous one)

(14) 15, 21 (Triangular numbers, the last difference was 5 and the subsequent 6.)

Finding the Nth term of an arithmetical sequence:

Example 1:

Consider the sequence 2, 4, 6, 8, 10, __ , __ , ___ ,

If we want to find a general formula for this sequence we can write it as 2n. 2n is the right answer, since if n=1, we get 2 as the first number. If n=2, we get: $2 \times 2 = 4$ as the second number, if n=4, we get 8 as the fourth number and so on. All we have to do is to substitute the appropriate number for n to get the relevant number in the sequence. So the 50th term is $2 \times 50 = 100$.

Working out formula for sequences:

This time consider a general arithmetical sequence as shown:

a, a +d, a+2d, a +3d, a+4d, a+5d, a+6d, ...

We can see that the second term is a+d

The third term is a+2d

The fourth term is a+3d

The fifth term is a+4d or a +(5-1)d

The sixth term is a+5d or a +(6-1)d

The seventh term is a+6d or a +(7-1)d

So the nth term is a+(n-1)d

You can check to see if this is right by substituting n=1, 2, 3, 4, 5 and so on to the appropriate numbers in the sequence. See example below:

Example: Find the nth term of the arithmetical sequence below:

5, 9, 13, 17, …

This is an arithmetical or linear sequence since the numbers go up by the same constant number. We know the nth term is a +(n - 1)d

In this case a=5 (This is the first term) d = 4 (this is the common difference between each successive number)

So, the nth term is $5 +(n – 1)\times 4 = 5 +4n –4 =4n +1$,

Formula to find the nth term of a geometric sequence:

This can be usually expressed as:

a, ar, ar^2, ar^3, …

Where a is the first term and r is the common ratio between two consecutive terms. The nth term for this would be ar^{n-1}

See example below which will make the formulae above a bit easier to follow.

Example: Find the 8th term of the sequence: 1, 3, 9, 27, 81, …

(You can see that the first term is 1 and the common ratio is 3, in other words each consecutive number is 3× the previous number)

The nth term is ar^{n-1}, Hence to find the 8th term we substitute the values for a and r in the formula ar^{n-1} which gives us: $1\times 3^{8-1} = 3^7 =$ 3×3×3×3×3×3×3 =2187. So the 8th term of this sequence has the value 2187

Chapter 8: Perimeters and Volumes of common shapes

Consider the shapes below:

(1) Rectangle

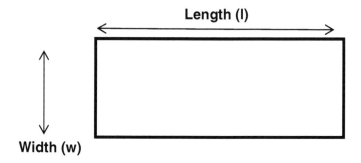

Length (l)

Width (w)

Area of a rectangle = Length × Width or l × w

Perimeter of a rectangle = 2l + 2w (distance around the rectangle)

Note: Area is measured in units squared, e.g. cm^2 or m^2 and perimeter (distance all round a shape) is measured in the appropriate units e.g. cm or m

---

Question based on areas

Example 1: Find the area and perimeter of a rectangle whose length is 12 cm and width is 5cm

Method: Area of a rectangle = l × w = 12 × 5 = 60 cm^2.

Perimeter = 2l + 2w = 2×12 +2×5 = 24 + 10 =34 cm. **Note:** For a square the length and width are obviously the same so the formula simplifies to l×l for the area and 4l for the perimeter, where l is the length of each side of the square

Example 2: Find the area of a square whose sides are 1m. Give your answer in cm^2

Area of square in metres squared = 1×1 = 1 m^2, but 1 m = 100cm.

So area in cm^2 = 100×100 =10000 cm^2

---

(2) Triangle

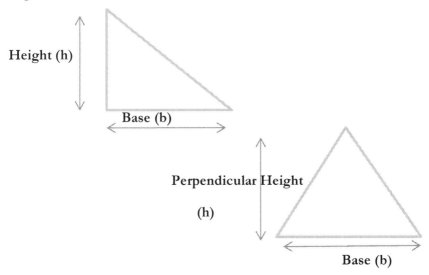

Area of a triangle $=\frac{1}{2} \times$ **base** $\times$ **height or** $\frac{1}{2}$**bh (The height is the perpendicular height relative to the base)**

Example: Find the area of a triangle whose base is 5m and height is 8m

Method: Area of a triangle $= \frac{1}{2} \times$ base $\times$ height

Substituting the values for base and height we get Area $= \frac{1}{2} \times 5 \times 8 =$

$\frac{1}{2} \times 40 = 20$ m^2

(3) Circle

Area of a circle is πr^2 (this means the value of π(pi) multiplied by radius squared)

Circumference of a circle (distance all the way round a circle) $= 2\pi r$ or πd

$2\pi r = 2 \times \pi$(pi)) $\times$ radius or $\pi \times$diameter

Note: Diameter of a circle $= 2 \times$ Radius

$\pi = 3.14$ **(approximately)**

(4) Cuboid (or a box)

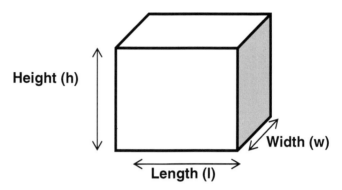

Height (h)

Width (w)

Length (l)

Volume of a cuboid is Height × Length × Width or V = h×l×w (units cubed e.g. cm^3 or m^3, etc)

Example: Find volume of a box whose width =3m, length =5m and height = 6m

Method: Volume of a cuboid (box) = h×l×w = 6×5×3 =30×3 = 90 m^3

Chapter 9:   Data Interpretation

Mean, Median, Mode and Range

First consider the different types of 'averages'.

That is Mean, Median, Mode and Range (You can try to remember these as: MMMR)

Mean: The sum of the numbers in a data set divided by the number of values in the Set

Median: The middle number of a data set when listed in order

Mode: The most frequently occurring number or numbers in a data set

Range: The difference between the highest and the smallest numbers in a data set

Example 1:
Find the mean value of the following data set:
2, 7, 1, 1, 7, 8, 9

Method: Find the sum first
$2 + 7 + 1 + 1 + 7 + 8 + 9 = 35$
Now divide this total by 7, since this is the total number of numbers
So, $35/7 = 5$
Hence, the mean value of this data set is 5

Example 2:
Find the median of 3, 7, 1, 8, and 6

Method: First re-order from smallest to biggest, re-writing the numbers we have:
1, 3, 6, 7, 8
Clearly the middle number is 6.
Hence, the median is 6

Example 3:
Find the median of 3, 6, 7, 1, 8 and 5

Method
First re-arrange to get 1, 3, 5, 6, 7, 8
Notice, in this case the middle number is between 5 & 6

So the median is $(5 + 6)/2 = 5.5$

Example 4:
Find the Range of the data set 3, 5, 7, 1, 8, and 11

Method: Find the difference between the biggest and smallest numbers
So the Range $= 11 - 1 = 10$

Example 5:
Find the Mode of the following numbers:
1, 4, 4, 4, 7, 8, 9, 9, 11, 12

Method: Find the most frequently occurring number. The most frequently occurring number is 4.
Hence the Mode is 4

Example 6:
Find the mode of 1, 3, 3, 3, 3 5, 5, 5, 5, 8, 8, 9

Method: As before find the most frequently occurring number(s).
Clearly there are two modes here. Both '3' and '5' occur most frequently, the same number of times, so we say this is a bi-modal distribution. That is, a distribution with two modes, namely 3 and 5

More examples:

Example 1:

The set of data below is the result in a class maths test showing the marks out of 10 for a group of 27 pupils. The teacher wants to find (1) the mode and (2) the mean mark for this test.

Maths marks	No of pupils (frequency)	No. of pupils × maths marks (frequency × marks)	
9	0	0 × 9 = 0	
8	1	1 × 8 = 8	
7	2	2 × 7= 14	
6	5	5 × 6 = 30	
5	8	8 × 5 = 40	
4	7	7 × 4 = 28	
3	4	4× 3 = 12	
2	0	0 × 2 = 0	
1	0	0 × 1 = 0	
Totals	27	0+8+14+30+40+28+12+0+0=132	

(1) The mode is simply the most frequently occurring mark. In this case it is 5 marks

 (Since 8 pupils get this, clearly it is the most common result)

(2) To work out the mean we need to work out the sum of all (pupils X marks) and divide it by the total number of pupils as shown below:

Sum all (pupils × marks) as shown above =132

The total number of pupils who took the test is 27

The mean mark in this test was thus $132 \div 27 = 4.9$ (to 1 decimal place)

Example 2:

The set of data below shows GCSE grade results in a particular subject for a group of 25 pupils in 2010 in a certain school.

B	A	C	A	A*
C	D	D	G	C
B	C	G	E	C
F	G	A	C	B
C	B	D	B	C

In addition point scores for each grade are as shown

A*	A	B	C	D	E	F	G
58	52	46	40	34	28	22	16

The Head teacher asked the responsible teacher to find out what the mean point score was and to compare it to the mode.

Method

See working out in the table and below

Step1: Work out the frequencies (the number of pupils) getting a particular grade, simply add up the number of times that particular grade occurs in the set of data given **above**. So for example there was only 1 occurrence of A*, there were 3 occurrences of Grade A, 5 occurrences of Grade B and so on.

Grades	A*	A	B	C	D	E	F	G
Point Score	58	52	46	40	34	28	22	16
Frequency (Number of students achieving this grade)	1	3	5	8	3	1	1	3
Frequency × Point Score	58×1 = 58	52×3 =156	46×5 =230	40×8 =320	34×3 =102	28×1 =28	22×1 =22	16×3 =48

Step2: Work out Frequency × point score for each grade as shown in the last row.

Step3: Add up all the Frequency × point score values, 58 +156 +230 +320 +102 +28 +22 +48 = 964

Step4: To work out the mean simply divide 948 by the total frequency (total number of pupils)

So 964÷25 = 38.6

The mean point score is approximately 39 (rounded to the nearest unit). This value shows that the average grade by this measure is approaching C.

However, the mode (most frequently occurring grade) is in fact a grade C, since 8 pupils got this.

You can see that if the school represented its data as a modal value (mode), then the grade appears slightly better than if it uses the mean!

Pie Charts

When data is represented in a circle this is called a pie chart. Basically you need to remember that a full circle or 360 degrees represents all the data (or 100% of the data). Half a circle or 180 degrees represents half the data (or 50% of the data), and similarly 25% of the data is represented by 90 degrees or a quarter of a circle. Essentially, each sector or slice of the pie chart shows the proportion of the total data in that category.

Example 1:

The pie chart below shows the percentage of applicants who got different grades in a psychometric aptitude test when applying for a job in a particular company. The requirement to be short listed for a second interview was to pass with high marks. If 140 applicants took this test how many of them were short listed?

Method: As illustrated the results in this aptitude test for this particular company show that 25% got the required 'high marks' to be short listed for a second

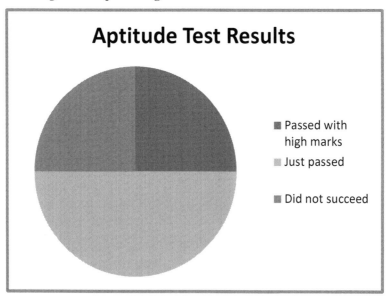

interview. Since a quarter of a circle corresponds to 25%. This means a quarter of the 140 applicants attained this which corresponds to 35 people.

Example 2:

The destination of 120 pupils who leave year 11 in School B in 2012 is represented in the pie chart below. The numbers outside the sectors represent the number of pupils

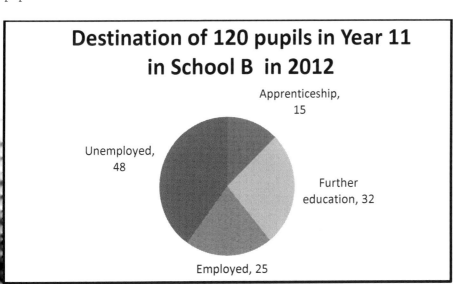

Destination of 120 pupils in Year 11 in School B in 2012

Apprenticeship, 15

Unemployed, 48

Further education, 32

Employed, 25

(1) What is the percentage of pupils who are unemployed?

Method:

The number of pupils out of 120 that are unemployed is 48. So the percentage of pupils who are unemployed is $\frac{48}{120} \times 100 = \frac{4800}{120} = \frac{480}{12} = 40\%$

(2) What fraction of pupils go on to Further Education?

Method:

The fraction of pupils that go on to further education is $\frac{32}{120} = \frac{8}{30} = \frac{4}{15}$, the fraction representing this in its simplest form is $\frac{4}{15}$

(3) What percentage of pupils is either employed or in apprenticeships? Give your answer to one decimal place?

Method:

Total number of pupils who are either in employment or apprenticeships =
25+15 =40, hence the percentage is $\frac{40}{120} \times 100 = \frac{4}{12} \times 100 = \frac{1}{3} \times 100 = 33.3\%$

Example 3:

Key Stage 3 results in English in two adjacent areas A and B are shown in the pie charts below. Area A recorded the results of 840 pupils and area B recorded the results of 900 pupils in this subject. The pie charts show the percentages obtained in the appropriate levels at KS3. How many more pupils obtained level 7 in area B compared to those gaining level 7 in area A?

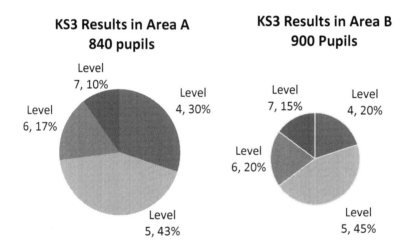

Method: The percentage of pupils who get level 7 in area A is 10%. This means 10% of 840 pupils get this level. 10% of 840 = $\frac{10}{100} \times 840 = 84$ pupils.

Similarly in area B, 15% of 900 pupils get level 7.

15% of 900 = $\frac{15}{100} \times 900$ = 135 pupils. This means area B has 135 – 84 more pupils = 51 more pupils who get level 7 compared to A

Bar charts

Bar charts can be represented in columns or as horizontal bars. They can be either simple bar charts that show frequencies associated with data values or they can be multiple bar charts to allow for comparisons between data sets as shown below. The examples below illustrate some of the ways bar charts can be used to represent data.

Example 1: In a cosmetics shop the number of items that were sold for four top brands over a one month period were recorded as shown in the bar chart below.

(1) Which brand had the highest sales? **You can see from the column bar chart below that Brand D had the highest sales as 40 items of this brand were sold during one month, which is higher than any other brand**

(2) What was the proportion of sales for Brand D compared to the total? Give your answer as a fraction in its lowest terms. **The number of Brand A items sold were 20, Brand B were 35 and Brand C were 25 and as we saw earlier 40 items of Brand D were sold. This means the total number of cosmetic items sold during this one month period = 120. Since 40 items belonged to Brand D,** compared to the total this is $\frac{40}{120}$ which simplifies to $\frac{1}{3}$

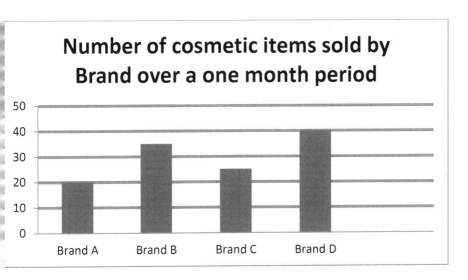

Example 2:

The bar chart below shows the amount of time in hours John, Bob and Bill spend surfing the web at weekends. What is the mean time per boy that is spent surfing the web at the weekend?

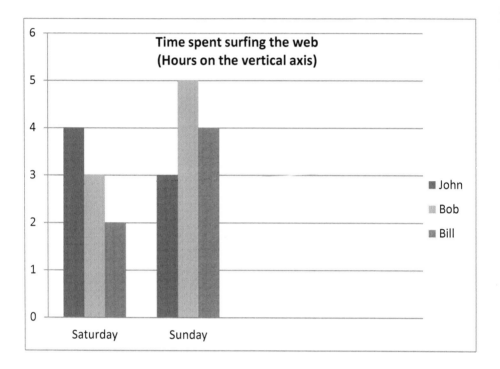

Method: John spends 4 hours on Saturday and 3 hours on a Sunday: a total of 7 hours

Bob spends a total of 3 hours on Saturday and 5 hours on Sunday: a total of 8 hours

Similarly, Bill spends a total of 2 + 4 = 6 hours on a weekend

Total time spent surfing between the 3 boys on a week end is 7+ 8 + 6 =21hours

Hence the mean time spent per boy is 21 ÷ 3 =7 hours

Example 3: Horizontal Bar Chart

In an on-line company the percentage of employees in 4 key departments is shown below. (1) If there are 560 employees altogether, how many are in the On-line marketing department? (2) How many more employees are there in On-line

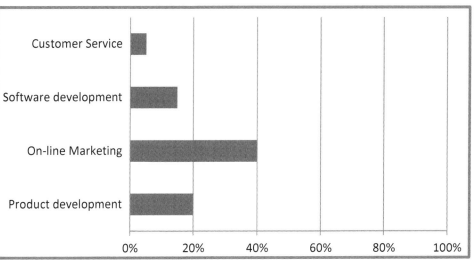

marketing compared to Customer Service department?

Percentage of employees in different departments in an online company

Method:

(1) From the bar chart you can see that 40% of the employees are in on-line marketing. Since there are 560 employees altogether, this means 40% of 560 = 224 employees
(10% of 560 =56, hence 40% = 4×56 = 4×50 + 4×6 = 200 + 24 = 224)

(2) 5% of employees are in customer service. Since there are 560 employees altogether, 10% = 56 and 5% =28 employees. We know from the previous question that there are 224 employees in On-line marketing. 224 – 28 = 196 employees. This means there are 196 more employees in the On-line marketing department compared to the Customers Service Department.

Example 4:

This composite bar chart below shows the percentage of pupils in a particular school who take and do not take additional lessons in music and maths respectively. What is the proportion of pupils who take extra music lessons? Give your answer as a fraction in its lowest terms.

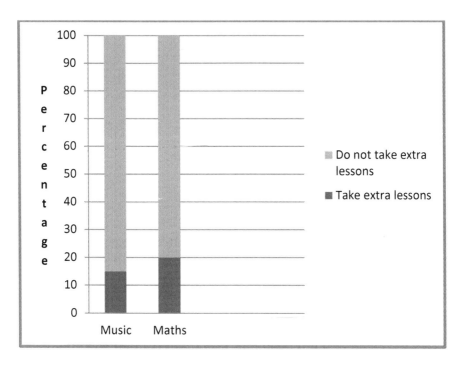

Method: The proportion of pupils who take extra music lessons is 15%. This is $\frac{15}{100}$ which simplifies to $\frac{3}{20}$. Hence $\frac{3}{20}$ of the pupils take extra lessons in music.

Example 5:

The composite bar chart below shows the number of cartons of Orange Juice, Pineapple Juice and Mango Juice sold in a local Supermarket on a given Saturday, Sunday and Monday. The vertical axis represents the number of fruit juice cartons sold.

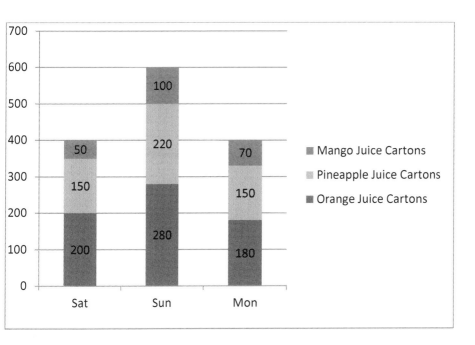

(Although a composite bar chart consists of single bars, these bars are split into two or more sections. These sections show the frequencies of the appropriate categories. Frequency in the above example is the different number of fruit cartons sold on different days.)

Example 1: On which day did this supermarket sell the highest number of mango juice cartons?

Clearly by looking at the composite graph you can see that on Sunday 100 cartons of Mango Juice were sold which is more than sold on Saturday or Monday.

Example 2: What was the proportion of pineapple juice cartons sold compared to the total of all drinks on all three days.

Method: Total Pineapple Juice cartons = 150 +220 +150 =520. Total of all three drinks sold = 400 (on Sat) + 600 (on Sun) and 400 (on Mon) = 1400 cartons of drinks.

So the proportion of pineapple cartons sold = **520÷1400 = 52÷140 =26÷70**

Or, $\dfrac{13}{35}$

Scatter Graphs

Scatter graphs or diagrams are used to show the type of relationship between two variables, for example height and weight, maths and physics scores, reading scores and IQ and so on. It also gives information on the type of correlation between the two variables.

Positive Correlation

This means when the value of one variable increases so does the value of the other one as shown in the example below.

A certain number of pupils' test marks in maths and physics are plotted. (The straight line drawn is called the line of best fit.) . You can see in this case there is a positive correlation between Maths marks and Physics marks.

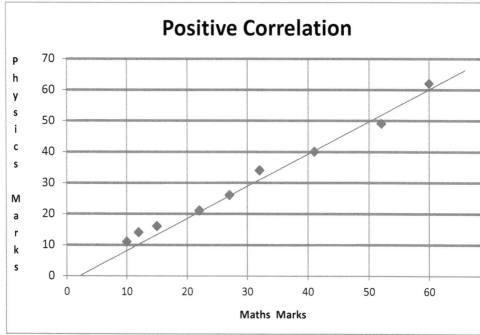

(1) How many pupils get more than 45 marks both in Maths and Physics?

Answer: 2 pupils get above 45 marks in both these subjects.

Method: look at the horizontal and vertical axis and draw an imaginary line at 45. Above 45 marks in both subjects you can see the record of two pupils.

(2) How many pupils get less than 20 marks in both Maths and Physics?

Answer: 3 pupils get less than 20 marks (using similar reasoning to the first answer)

Negative Correlation

This means that as one variable decreases in value the other one increases.

Example of Negative correlation:

This time some pupils' scores in Maths were plotted with their scores in History. It appears that in this particular case there was a negative correlation between Maths and History scores as shown below.

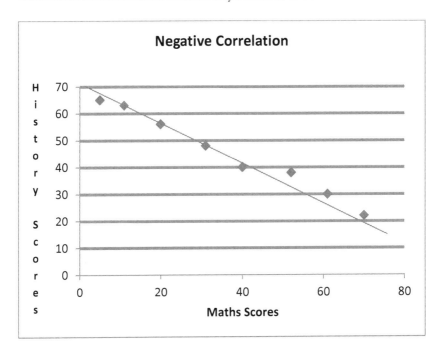

Another example of a negative correlation is the one between the price of a car and its age. As a car gets older its price is generally lower.

Zero Correlation

This is when there is no relationship between the two variables. The points are scattered all over the place so that we cannot really draw a line of best fit. For example consider the relationship between Science and English marks shown below in this particular example

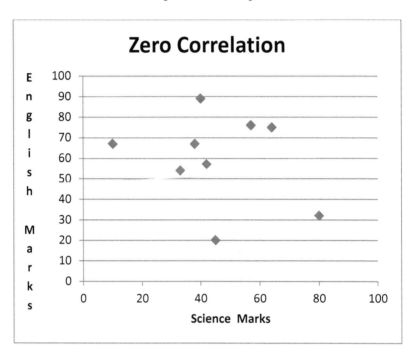

(1) In the example above what was the approximate mark in Science for the pupil who scored 20 marks in English?

Answer: 45 is the approximate mark in Science

Method: From the vertical axis, go along the horizontal line at 20 marks, this corresponds to approximately 45 marks in Science

It is worth remembering that we can have a weak positive correlation or a weak negative correlation. For example the percentage of men with grey hair is only weakly correlated with increasing age!

An example of scatter graph that shows a weak positive correlation, for example between Geography marks and History marks

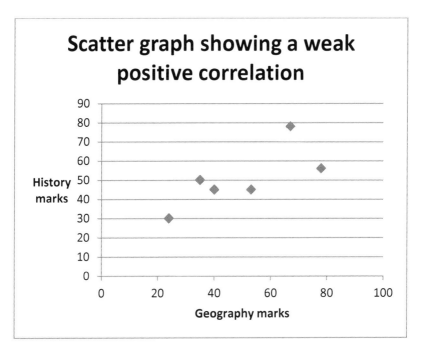

Scatter graph showing a weak positive correlation

Finally, just for interest it is worth remembering the difference between correlation and causation. For example the incidence of heart attacks is correlated with high total cholesterol, but it is worth noting that many people with high cholesterol do not have a heart attack. In fact, the incidence of heart attacks is correlated with total cholesterol, LDL, triglycerides, obesity, body mass index and genetic factors. In other words, in this case the incidence of heart disease is multifactorial (has many factors that are responsible) and to draw a causal link from one factor may be erroneous. Another interesting and controversial issue is that more vaccinations have resulted in a higher incidence of autism! Unfortunately, as vaccination rates went up in the USA so did the rates of autism. This led some people to falsely attribute vaccinations as the cause of autism. Autism has gone up for other reasons, more awareness leading to more diagnostic cases, genetic factors which we were not previously aware of and so on. Often there are other 'variables' involved. Unfortunately, journalists and sometimes even scientists jump to 'causal' conclusions. In higher level statistics there are methodologies of significance testing which help ascertain whether a correlation is likely to be 'causal' or whether there could be other factors at play.

Line graph

A line graph is a way to represent two sets of related data. **It is often used to show trends**

Example 1: The data below shows the percentage of candidates who had 'A' level mathematics who were short-listed for the first interview when applying to a consultancy company. This data is shown in the table below. However, the same data can be shown as a line graph that follows.

Year	2005	2006	2007	2008	2009	2010
% of candidates with 'A' level Maths	26%	35%	45%	37%	48%	32%

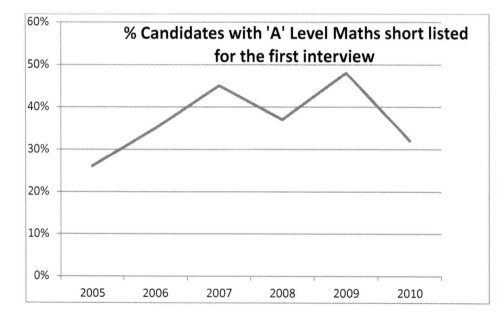

What was the change in percentage points for candidates that were short-listed between 2008 and 2010?

Method: You can see from the table as well as the graph that the success rate actually dropped from (approx.) 37% to (approx) 32%. That is decreased by 5% points.

Example 2:

The sales of Company A and Company B are plotted in a line graph from 2001 to 2006. If 850 employees worked for Company A and 800 employees worked for Company B in 2006. What was the sales per employee for Company B in 2006?

Sales of Company A and Company B from 2001 - 2006 in £ million

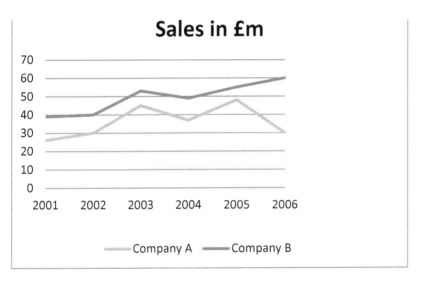

Method: From the line graph it can be seen that in 2006, Company B had a sales of £60 million. If 800 employees worked for this company, then clearly the sales per employee was £60,000,000 ÷ 800 = 600,000÷8 = 300,000÷4 =150,000÷2 = £75000. Hence, the sales per employee in Company B in 2006 was £75000.

Cumulative Frequency diagrams

Example

A class test in maths was marked out of 70. The table below shows the distribution of marks among 20 pupils.

Marks (Max 70 marks)	Number of Pupils (frequency)	Cumulative Frequency (keep adding the frequencies)
1 - 10	0	0
11 - 20	2	0 + 2 = 2
21 - 30	3	2 + 3 = 5
31 - 40	5	5 + 5 = 10
41 - 50	5	10 + 5 =15
51 - 60	4	15 + 4 =19
61 - 70	1	19 +1 =20

From the graph you can see the median (half way up the cumulative frequency is 10) this corresponds to 40 marks. This means half the students get up to 40 marks and half get over 40 marks.

(Just for your information when plotting the graph one plots the upper bound of the mark with the corresponding cumulative frequency value. So for example in the mark range 21- 30 you plot 30 (the upper bound) with 5(the cumulative frequency)

Now see if you can follow the answers to the questions below

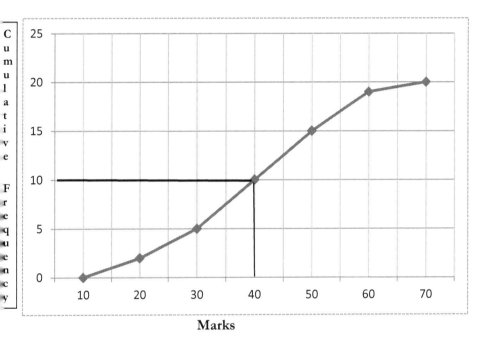

Marks

(1) What mark corresponds to the lower quartile?

The lower quartile is a quarter of the way up the cumulative frequency axis. This corresponds to 5. The total cumulative frequency is 20, so a quarter on this axis is at 5. If you draw a horizontal line at 5 until it meets the curve and then draw the corresponding vertical line at this point it meets the horizontal line at 30. This means 25% of the pupils score 30 marks or below.

(2) What marks correspond to the upper quartile?

The upper quartile is three quarters of the way up the cumulative frequency axis. Three quarters of 20 (the total cumulative frequency) is 15. This corresponds to 50 marks on the horizontal axis.

This means that 25% of the pupils get more than 50 marks.

(3) What is the Inter Quartile Range (IQR)?

This is simply the difference between the Upper Quartile and the Lower Quartile.

IQR = Upper Quartile − Lower Quartile

IQR = 50 - 30 = 20

Summary

To find Median: From the vertical axis (which represents the cumulative frequency) go up to 50% or half way up this axis and draw a horizontal line to the cumulative frequency curve, then draw a vertical line at this point to meet the horizontal axis and read off the appropriate value

To find the Upper Quartile go up the 75% mark vertically (three quarters of the way up) and similarly read the corresponding value on the horizontal axis.

To find the Lower Quartile go up the 25% mark vertically (one quarter of the way up) and read the corresponding value on the horizontal axis

To find the Inter Quartile Range simply take the difference the Upper Quartile and the Lower Quartile.

Two way tables

These are used to compare data between two variables. For example, comparing the different modes of transport (one variable) used by different schools (second variable), say inner city schools and suburban schools. Example 1 demonstrates this.

Example 1:

		Method of Transport			
		Car	Bus	Walking	Other
Type of Schools	**Inner City**	28%	32%	24%	16%
	Suburban	62%	18%	12%	8%

From the data above you can see that 32% of children take the bus in Inner City schools compared to 18% who take the bus in suburban schools. Similarly, 62% of pupils in suburban schools arrive by car as compared to 28% in inner city schools. You can also compare other modes of transport between the two schools.

Example 2:

This second example shows a two way table comparing pupil results for GCSE History with GCSE Geography grades.

Geography GCSE grades	History GCSE Grades								
	A*	A	B	C	D	E	F	G	Total
A*		1	2	1					4
A									
B		1	2	3					6
C		2	3	4	2				11
D			2	3	1	1			7
E				2	1	1	1		5
F									
G									
Total		4	9	13	4	2	1		33

Typical questions

(1) How many pupils achieved a grade B in both History and Geography?

Method: Look down the vertical column (History) with Grade B and see where it crosses the horizontal row (Geography) with the same Grade. You can see that the cell that corresponds to both these being true is 2. So 2 pupils get a B in both History & Geography.

(2) How many pupils get a C in History?

Method: If you look down the vertical column (History) at grade C, you can see that the total pupils who get a grade C in History is 13.

(3) How many pupils achieved a grade C or above in Geography?

Method: Look at the horizontal row (Geography) and see how many got C, B, A and A* (that is C or above). If you look at the horizontal cells corresponding to these grades the totals are 11 for grade C, 6 for grade B, 0 for grade A and 4 for grade A*. This corresponds to a final total of 11+6+0+ 4 = 21. This means 21 pupils got a C grade or above in Geography.

(4) What is the percentage of pupils who got a grade B in History? Give the answer correct to 1 decimal place.

Method: Look down the vertical column (History) at grade B. The total number of pupils who got grade B in History is 9. Since 33 pupils took the exam altogether, the percentage of pupils who got a grade B in History is $(9/33) \times 100 = 27.27\%$ which is 27.3% to 1 decimal place.

Chapter 10: Basic Algebra

The word 'algebra' comes from the Arabic al-jebr, which means 'the reuniting of broken parts'. By implication this means the equating of like to like.

In algebra we often use letters instead of numbers. There are some basic conventions and rules of algebra that you should be familiar with to progress in this subject. This chapter will be useful for you if you have forgotten your algebra.

If you see	We Mean
$x = y$	x equals y
$x > y$	x is greater than y
$x < y$	x is less than y
$x \geq y$	x is greater than or equal to y
$x \leq y$	x is less than or equal to y
$x + y$	the sum of x and y
$x - y$	subtract y from x
xy	x times y
x/y	x divided by y
$x \div y$	x divided by y
x^n	x to the power n
$x(x + y)$	x times the sum of x + y

Also note that:

$$x(x + y) = x^2 + xy$$

$$x^2(x + x^2 + y) = x^3 + x^4 + x^2y$$

In general, $a \times a \times a \times a \ldots\ldots(n \text{ times}) = a^n$

You also need to know these algebraic rules for the multiplication and division of positive and negative numbers.

Multiplying positive and negative numbers.

$(+) \times (+) = +$ (a plus number times a plus number gives us a plus number)

$(+) \times (-) = -$ (a plus number times a minus number gives us a minus number)

$(-) \times (+) = -$ (a minus number times a plus number gives us a minus number)

$(-) \times (-) = +$ (a minus number times a minus number gives us a plus number)

Dividing positive and negative numbers.

$(+) \div (+) = +$ (a plus number divided by a plus number gives us a plus number)

$(+) \div (-) = -$ (a plus number divided by a minus number gives us a minus number)

$(-) \div (+) = -$ (a minus number divided by a plus number gives us a minus number)

$(-) \div (-) = +$ (a minus number divided by a minus number gives us a plus number)

Summary: <u>For both multiplication and division, like signs gives us a plus sign and unlike signs gives a minus sign</u>

Also when adding and subtracting it is worth knowing that:

When you add two minus numbers you get a bigger minus number.

Example 1: $-4 - 6 = -10$

When you add a plus number and a minus number you get the sign corresponding to the bigger number as shown below:

Example 2: $+6 - 9 = -3$, whereas, $-6+9 = 3$

When you subtract a minus from a plus or minus number you need to note the results as shown below:

Example 3: $6 -(-3)$ we get $6+3 = 9$ (since $-(-3) = +3$)

Example 4: $7 -(+3)$ we get $7 - 3 = 4$ (since $-(+3) = -3$)

In this case note that $-(-) = +$. Also, $+(-) = -$ and $-(+) = -$.

Remember the BIDMAS rule you were introduced to earlier which specifies the rules concerning the order in which you carry out arithmetical operations:

Simplifying algebraic expressions

Example 1: Simplify $3x +4x +5x$

Method: We simple add up all the x's.

Hence we get $3x+4x+5x = 12x$

Example 2: Simplify $3x +4x +3y +5y$

Method: Add up all the like terms.

So we get $3x+4x +3y+5y = 7x +8y$

(Notice we add up all the x's and then all the y's)

Example 3: Simplify $3m +4y +2m -3y$

Method: as before, we add and subtract like terms.

Now $3m+2m =5m$ and $4y-3y =1y$ or just y.

So we can write $3m +4y +2m -3y = 5m + y$.

Multiplying out brackets.

Example 1: Expand $3(2x +5)$

Method: we multiply 3 by each term in the bracket. So we get $3 \times 2x + 3 \times 5$ which gives us $6x + 15$.

Example 2: Expand and simplify $3(2x +5) +4(2x+7)$

Method: Multiply 3 by each term in the first bracket then 4 by each term in the second bracket. The final step is to simplify by collecting up the like terms.

$3(2x+5) +4(2x+7) =6x+15+8x+28 =14x + 43$

Notice the last step is simply adding $6x + 8x$ and then $15+28$.

Algebraic Substitution

This is the process of substituting numbers for letters and working out the value of the corresponding expression.

Example 1: if a $=5$ and b$=6$ work out $2a +3b$

Method: Substitute numbers for letters and we get:

$2 \times 5+3 \times 6$

(Notice 2a means $2 \times a$ and 3b means $3 \times b$)

So, $2 \times 5 +3 \times 6 = 10+18 =28$

This means that $2a+3b =28$

Example 2: If m=7 and n=8 work out 5m– 3n

Substituting numbers for letters we get:

$5 \times 7 - 3 \times 8 = 35 - 24 = 11$

So 5m –3n =11

Simple Equations

Consider the following English statements and their mathematical equivalent:

English Statements	Algebra
Something plus five equals ten	$x + 5 = 10$
Something times two, plus five equals eleven	$2x + 5 = 11$
Something times three, minus five equals thirteen	$3x - 5 = 13$
Something divided by two equals three	$x/2 = 3$

Now consider solving these equations using a common sense approach.

Example 1: Something plus five equals ten. What is 'something'?

Clearly we need to add five to five to get ten. So 'something' in this case equals five.

Solving this by algebra can be very similar. As we saw, we can re-write the English statement above in algebra as follows:

$x + 5 = 10$ (notice, we are representing 'something' by x)

Now, if $x + 5 = 10$ clearly x (which represents 'something') is equal to 5.

So, $x = 5$

Example 2: 'Something' times two plus five equals eleven. Find the 'something'.

We know that 'something' times two plus five equals eleven.

So the two times 'something' must equal 6. In which case 'something' must be 3.

Now consider the algebraic equivalent.

$2x + 5 = 11$

This means $2x = 6$

Which means $x = 3$

Now consider a more formal method.

Imagine an equation like a balance. Whatever you do to one side you must do to the other.

Example 3: Solve the equation $x + 5 = 10$

Subtract 5 from both sides

So, $x = 5$

However, we can also use the method of taking inverses.

The rules are: When something is added to the x-term subtract, when something is subtracted from the x-term then add. When x, is multiplied, by a number we divide. Finally, when the x-term, is divided, by a number we multiply.

Example 1:

Two people collect the same amount of money each for a charity. The fund raising organisation adds £500.50 and the total amount they collect including their contribution is £1100.70. How much does each person collect?

To solve this algebraically, let the amount each person collect be x. This means $2x + £500.50 = £1100.70$ (2 times the amount each person collects plus the £500.50 the fund raising organisation contributes = £1100.70)

In the equation, $2x + 500.50 = 1100.70$, we now have to Subtract 500.50 from both sides, So we are left with $2x = 600.20$

Now divide both sides by 2(that is, take the inverse of X2)

So, $x = £300.10$, This means each person collects £300.10

Example 2:

John has £22 more than Brian. Altogether they have £68. How much do they each have?

Let the amount Brian has be £x

Since Brian's amount plus John's amount = £68, we can write algebraically that $x + x + 22 = 68$.

Simplifying this expression we get $2x + 22 = 68$

Subtracting 22 from both sides we get:

$2x = 46$, now divide both sides by 2. We get $x = 23$

Hence Brian has £23, and John has £45

Example 3: (Simultaneous equations where you have two unknowns in this case)

The sum of two numbers is 30. Their difference is 12. What are the two numbers?

Method: Let one of the numbers be x and the other y.

So we can deduce that (1) x + y = 30 and (2) x – y = 12.

If you add the left **and** right hand sides of the two equations then we can eliminate y. That is x + y + x –y = 30 + 12. This simplifies to 2x = 42, or x =21. Now that we have found x, we can substitute for x in the first equation. i.e. (1) to give us 21 + y = 30. By subtracting 21 from both sides we can find that y = 9. Hence the two numbers are 21 and 9.

Practice Tests

There are five practice tests to help you become more proficient during the real test(s). The first test is relatively easy and is just to make sure you remember your basic maths. The subsequent tests are slightly harder and are more typical of the type of questions you are likely to get at an intermediate level and advanced level. Remember advanced numerical reasoning tests don't involve complex mathematics. The fourth test is typical of data interpretation tests you might get for a professional career track. Finally, the last test consists of word problems which can be solved using basic algebra. For graduate entry typical of Tests 2, 3, 4 and 5 try to achieve 10 questions out of 15 correct (this works out at approximately 67%). For entry into civil service, banking and consultancy careers try to get 12 out of 15 questions correct, that is 80% all within the time limits set. Each practice test has 15 questions.

Practice Test 1 – 15 Minutes

(No calculators allowed)

(1) Work out 27 × 17

(2) Find 15% of £300

(3) What is 124 ÷ 100

(4) What is 327 ÷ 0.1

(5) Find $2\frac{3}{4}$ of 460

(6) If I travel 60km in 2.5 hours, what is my average speed?

(7) There are 21 employees in a small company. Three of them go on a special training course. What is the fraction of employees that do not go on this training course? Give your answer in its lowest terms.

(8) 2500 millilitres of liquid is divided into 20 containers. How many millilitres of liquid does each container have?

(9) A walking group walks 24 Km every week.

If 8km is approximately equal to 5 miles, estimate how many miles the weekly walk consist of?

(10) 18 people are asked to collect £3.50 each for a charity. All of them succeed. What is the total amount collected?

(11) A group activity consists of 16 tasks. Each task lasts 15 minutes. How many hours will this group activity last?

(12) A meeting begins at 10:50. There is a general introduction for 6 minutes, a power-point presentation for 18 minutes and finally a question and answer session for 26 minutes. When does the meeting end? Give your answer using the 24-hour clock.

(13) A company calculated that it had given bonuses to its junior and senior staff in the ratio of 1:3. There was a total of £68000 bonus given. Assuming there were 20 senior staff, how much did each member of the senior staff get?

(14) A teacher has to see 16 parents for 12 minutes each to discuss pupil progress. In addition there is a 25 minute break. How long does the parents' session last in hours and minutes?

(15) In a numerical reasoning test an applicant achieved 27 out of 45 marks. What was the percentage mark that the applicant received in this test?

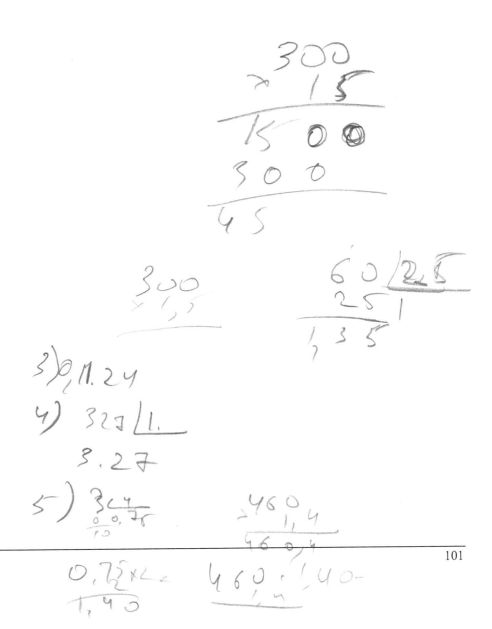

Answers to Test 1

1. $27 \times 17 = 459$
   Method $27 \times 17 = 27 \times 10 + 27 \times 5 + 27 \times 2 = 270 + 135 + 54 = 459$
2. 15% of £300 = £45
   Method: 10% = £30 & 5% = £15, Hence total = £45
3. $124 \div 100 = 1.24$
4. $327 \div 0.1 = 3270$ (remember when dividing by 0.1, you are effectively dividing by one tenth)
5. $2\frac{3}{4}$ of 460 = 1265
   Method: double 460 + half of 460 + a quarter of 460 = 920 + 230 + 115 = 1265
6. Average Speed = 24km/hour
   Method: Speed = Distance $\div$ Time = $60 \div 2.5 = 24$
7. The number of employees that do not go on a training course is $\frac{6}{7}$
   Method: Number of employees that do not go on a training course is 18. Hence fraction of employees that do not go $= \frac{18}{21}$ which simplifies to $\frac{6}{7}$ (Divide the top and bottom numbers of $\frac{18}{21}$ by 3
8. Each container has 125ml of liquid
   Method: $2500 \div 20 = 125$
9. The weekly walk consists of 15miles. Method: Since 8km = 5miles then 24 km $= 24 \times \frac{5}{8} = 120 \div 8 = 60 \div 4 = 15$
10. Total amount collected = £63
    Method: $18 \times 3 + 0.5 \times 18 = 54 + 9 = £63$
11. The group activity lasts for 4hours
    Method: $16 \times 15 = 16 \times 10 + 16 \times 5 = 160 + 80 = 240$ minutes = 4hrs

12. The meeting ends at 11:40

    Method: 6+ 18 + 26 = 50 minutes. Add 50 mins to 10:50 to get
    11:40

13. Each senior member gets £2550

    Method: Total parts in ratio = 4, therefore each part = 68000/4
    = £17000. Senior staff get 3× as much = £51000. Since there are
    20 senior staff each member of the senior staff gets £2550

14. The parents' session lasts 3 hours and 37 minutes

    Method: $16 \times 12 + 25$ (min break) = 192 +25 = 217 minutes
    Since 180 minutes = 3 hours, we are left with 37 minutes. Hence
    total time taken = 3 hours 37 minutes

15. 60%

    Method: The applicant received 27 marks out of 45

    Hence the percentage mark was $\frac{27}{45} \times 100 = 60\%$

Practice Test 2 – 20 minutes

(Calculators allowed)

(1) An employee attends a course which is 81.5 miles away. She is allowed to claim travel expenses for the journey there and back at 40p per mile. How much is the employee allowed to claim?

(2) A school organizes a day trip to the local museum. There are 48 pupils altogether. There is requirement for one adult per 8 pupils. What is the total number of people on this trip?

(3) A food retailer decides to pay 1.5% of its profits as bonuses to its frontline staff. In 2010 the retailer made 22 million pounds of profit. Assuming the retailer had 250 front line staff, how much approximately did each member of the staff receive in bonuses?

(4) A young couple bought a one bedroom flat in London for £180,000 at the beginning of 2005. The prices increased by 2% per annum from 2005 to 2012. What was the value of the house at the end of 2012. Give your answer to the nearest whole number.

(5) A meeting ends at 1425. The meeting was in two parts, starting with a presentation that lasted 30 minutes and ending with a discussion lasting 20 minutes. When did the meeting start?

(6) The ratio of male to female workers in company A is 4:5. Assuming there are 945 employees altogether, how many of the employees are male?

(7) A book store orders 80 fast selling books at £2.99 each. They sell each book at £6.70. How much profit will they make if they manage to sell all the books?

(8) A firm has a fund raising day for an educational charity they support. On average each employee contributes £4.75 towards this charity. 340 employees contributed this amount. How much is collected in total?

(9) Employees have access to a lawn area for general relaxation. The lawn is rectangular with a circular pool in the grounds. The lawn is 8.5m long and

4.5m wide. The pool has a radius of 1m. What is the area of the actual lawn that is available to the employees to the nearest whole number?

(10) A student scores 45 marks in a standardized test. After some weeks of additional tuition his scores improve by 30%. What marks does he now get in a similar test?

(11) What is 12.5% of 360 Kilograms?

(12) A company has 950 employees. They encourage employees to join a variety of fitness classes. 15% join a gym class, 32% join a yoga class, 11% join a jogging group and the rest do not join any group. How many employees do not join any fitness class?

(13) A walking trip was organized. The map showed a scale of 1:100000. The main organizer planned out the route as follows:

Start from A and going to B total distance on the map =2.7cm

From B to C the distance on the map was 3.2 cm

Finally the distance from C to D was 8.2 cm

What was the distance in Kilometres from A to D?

(14) The head of Marketing orders some books and DVD's for some new employees in a particular department for some training. He orders 92 set books at £1.65 each, 220 Notebooks which come in packs of 10 at £4.60 per pack, and 8 Basic Training DVD's at £5.75 each. There is a Company discount of 12% on the total order. Calculate the total amount the order cost after the discount. Give your answer correct to 2 decimal places.

(15) In a year 11 group, there are 54 pupils altogether of which 24 are girls. Music lessons are taken by $\frac{1}{5}$ of the boys and $\frac{1}{4}$ of the girls. What is the total number of pupils from the year 11 group that take music lessons?

Answers to Test 2

(1) £65.20

Method: Each way is 81.5 miles. So there are 163 miles which includes the return journey @ 40p per mile

$= 163 \times 40p = £163 \times 0.4 = £65.20$

(2) 54

Method: There are 48 pupils altogether. 1 adult per 8 pupils means 6 adults are needed. (Since $48 \div 8 = 6$). This means there are a total of 48 + 6 people = 54 people on this trip.

(3) £1,320

Method: 1% of £22,000,000 (£22M) = £220,000

This means ½% = £110,000. Hence 1% + ½ % = £330,000

Since there are 250 front line staff, each member of the front line staff gets $330,000 \div 250 = 33000 \div 25 = 6600 \div 5 = £1,320$

(4) £210,899 to the nearest pound

Method: From the beginning of 2005 to the end of 2012 consists of 8 years. If the price rises by 2% per annum for 8 consecutive years, then the price after 8 years is $180,000 \times (1.02)^8$. (Note that 1.02^8 means $1.02 \times 1.02 \times 1.02 \ldots$ up to 8 times) Hence £180,000 $\times 1.02^8 = 210898.69$ = £210,899 to the nearest pound.

(5) 13:35

Method: The presentation lasts 30 minutes and the Q&A session lasts 20 minutes. Hence the time taken for the meeting is 50 minutes. Since it ends at 14:25 we need to subtract 50 minutes from this to give us 13:35

(6) 420

Method: The ratio of male to female employees of 4:5 implies there are 9 parts in total. Since there are 945 employees in total, each part is equivalent to 105 employees. This means there are 420 male employees.

(7) £296.80

Method: Profit per book is £6.70 – 2.99 or we can say £6.71- £3 = £3.71. The profit for 10 books is £37.10, hence the profit for 80 books = £37.10 × 8 = £296.80

(Or else use a calculator)

(8) £1,615

Method: Total collected = £340 × 4.75 = £340×4 + £340×0.5 + £340×0.25 = £1360 + £170 + £85 = £1,615

(9) 35 m^2

Method: Lawn area available = area of rectangle – area of circular pond. Hence, lawn area available = 8.5×4.5 - πr^2 = 38.25 – 3.14×1×1 =38.25 – 3.14 = 35.11m^2 = 35m^2 to the nearest whole number

(10) 58.5 marks

Method: 30% of 45 = 45×0.3 = 13.5

We now need to add 13.5 to 45 to give us a total of 58.5 marks

(11) 45 kgm

Method: 12.5% = 10% + 2.5%

10% of 360 Kgm = 36, 5% =18 and 2.5% =9. So 10% +2.5% = 36 + 9 = 45kgm

(12) 399 employees

Method: Total percentage that join some fitness group = 15% + 32% + 11% = 58%. Hence 42% do not join any fitness group. 42% of 950 = 950×0.42 = 399

(13) 14.1 km

Method: Total distance on the map = 2.7 + 3.2 + 8.2 = 14.1 cm. Using a scale 1:100000. This means 14.1cm =14.1×100000cm =1410000cm = 14100 metres (divide1410000 by 100 to give the answer in metres). Finally, 14100 ÷1000 = 14.1 km

(14) £263.12

Method: Using a calculator

92 set books @ £1.65 each = £151.80, 220 notebooks in packs of 10 means 22 packs @ £4.60 each = £101.20, 8 training DVD's @ £5.75 each = £46. Total cost before discount = £151.80 + £101.20 + £46 = £299. Discount of 12% on £299 means the department pays £35.88 less

Hence actual amount paid for the order = £299 - £35.88 = £263.12

(15) 12 pupils

Method: There are 54 pupils altogether. 24 are girls, so 30 must be boys. Hence the number of pupils who take music lessons are: $\frac{1}{4}$ of 24 plus $\frac{1}{5}$ of 30 = 6 + 6 = 12 pupils.

Practice Test 3   Number Sequences (15 minutes – Calculators allowed)

Complete the following number sequences

(1) 7, 12 , 17 ,___ , ___

(2) 17, 26 , 37, 50, ___ , ___

(3) 3, 7, 15, 31, ___ , ___

(4) 0, 1, 1, 2, 3, 5, ___ , ___

(5) 50, 25, 12.5, ___ , ___

(6) 16, 24, 36, 54, ___ , ___

(7) 7, 27, 127, 627,___ , ___

(8) 64, 16, 4, ___ , ___

(9) 1, 9, 81, ___ , ___

(10) 2, 5, 12.5, 31.25, ___, ___

(11) 100, 50, 25, ___, ___

(12) 18, 13, 8, 3, ___, ___

(13) 7, 21, 63, 189, ___, ___

(14) Find the 10th term of the sequence 0.6, 0.45, 0.30, 0.15, ...

(15) Find the 50th term of the sequence, 12, 19, 26, 33, ...

Answers to Test 3

(1) 7, 12 , 17 ,**22, 27** (Increase each number by 5,)

(2) 17, 26, 37, 50, **65, 82** (The difference between consecutive numbers is: 9, 11, 13, **15 and 17.**)

(3) 3, 7, 15, 31, **63, 127** (the difference between consecutive numbers is double the previous one. Difference between 7 & 3 =4, between 15 & 7 =8, between 31 & 15 =16, between 63 & 31 = 32 and finally between 127 & 63 = 64)

(4) 0, 1, 1, 2, 3, 5, **8, 13** (Next number is sum of previous two)

(5) 50, 25, 12.5, **6.25, 3.125** (Halve the previous number)

(6) 16, 24, 36, 54, **81, 121.5** (Each consecutive number is 1.5× the previous number)

(7) 7, 27, 127, 627, **3127, 15627** (First number is $5^1 + 2$, Next number is $5^2 + 2$, hence the fifth number is $5^5 + 2 = 5×5×5×5×5 + 2 = 3127$ and the sixth number is $5^6 + 2 = 5×5×5×5×5×5 + 2 = 15627$)

(8) 64, 16, 4, **1, $\frac{1}{4}$** (Next number is a quarter of previous one)

(9) 1, 9, 81, **729, 6561** (Each consecutive number is 9× the previous one)

(10) 2, 5, 12.5, 31.25, **78.125, 195.3125** (the next number is 2.5× the previous number)

(11) 100, 50, 25, **12.5, 6.25** (Next number is half the previous number)

(12) 18, 13, 8, 3, **-2, -7** (Decrease each number by 5)

(13) 7, 21, 63, 189, **567, 1,701** (Multiply the previous number by 3)

(14) The 10th term of the sequence is **− 0.75**

Method: The nth term of the sequence is 0.75 -0.15n, since if n=1 them 0.75 -0.15×1 = 0.6, if n=2, 0.75 -0.15×2 = 0.45, hence the 10th term is 0.75 - 0.15×10 = 0.75 − 1.5 = -0.75

(15) The 50th term is: **355**

Method: The arithmetical sequence goes up by a value of 7 each time. Hence the Nth term is 7n + 5. (Check, if n=1, then 7n + 5 = 7×1+5 =12, If n = 2, then 7n +5 = 7×2 +5 = 19, and so on). Hence the 50th term is 7×50 + 5 =355

Practice Test 4

Data interpretation with Multiple Choice (Advanced Numerical Reasoning Test) – 30 minutes, Calculators allowed

Calculators allowed

Question 1

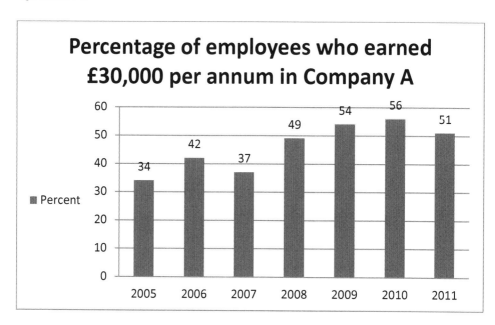

Percentage of employees who earned £30,000 per annum in Company A

(1) The mean percentage who earned £30,000 from 2008 to 2011 was:

(a) 20%   (b) 21%   (c) 37%   (d) 52.5%   (e) 24.5%

(2) What was the percentage increase in employees that earned £30,000 from 2005 to 2011?

(a) 26%   (b) 28%   (c) 17%   (d) 40%   (e)50%

Question 2

A teacher wanted to compare the progress of 8 pupils across two tests and see who had increased by at least 10 percentage points. The first test was out of 40 and the second test was out of 50. Which pupils meet this target?

Pupils	Test1 (marks out of 40)	Test 2 (marks out of 50)
A	22	32
B	25	32
C	17	27
D	25	35
E	19	26
F	12	20
G	25	34
H	30	47

(a) C, F & G   (b) C, E & G   (c) C, F & H (d) A, C & D

(e) A, B & G

Question 3

Report: <u>The number of emergency admissions at 4 Hospitals on three days in the UK</u>

Hospital	Friday	Saturday	Sunday
Hospital A	200	210	90
Hospital B	180	160	100
Hospital C	250	150	60
Hospital D	150	120	20

(1) Which hospital had the most admissions for all three days combined?

(a) Hospital B   (b) Hospital A   (c) Hospital D   (d) Hospital C

(2) What is the percentage of admissions in Hospital A on a Sunday compared to all Hospitals on the same day?

(a) 31.33%   (b) 29.33%   (c) 33.33%   (d) 40%   (e) 72%

Question 4

Report: E-Reader Sales in millions for March 2011

Country	Kindle	Ipad	Nook
USA	2	1.5	0.02
UK	0.5	0.3	0.01
Germany	0.4	0.35	0.02
France	0.35	0.45	0.03

(1) How many Nook e-readers in thousands were sold in Europe during this month?
   (a) 8000   (b) 80,000   (c) 81,000   (d) 810,000 (e) 60000

(2) Which country had the least Kindle and Ipad sales combined?

   (a) USA   (b) UK   (c) Germany   (d) France

Question 5

Annual sales report for 4 medium sized companies in 2010

Company	Annual Sales	Number of employees
A	£4 million	50
B	£6 million	100
C	£2.4 million	60
D	£8 million	160

(1) Which company had the highest sales per employee?

(a) Company A (b) Company B (c) Company C (d) Company D

(2) Company D had a 25% increase in sales in 2011. Also the number of employees increased by 40. What was the sales per employee in Company D in 2011?

 (a) £120,000   (b) £100,000 (c) £110,000 (d) £50,000 (e) £121,000

Question 6

The graph below shows the percentage of pupils achieving Grade C in Maths from 2006 to 2011.

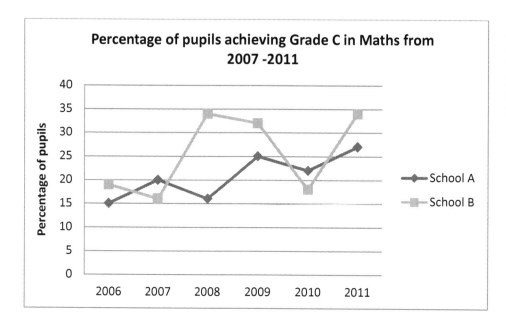

(1) By how many percentage points approximately did School B outperform School A in 2011?
   (a) 17%   (b) 7%   (c) 10%   (d) 15%   (e) 12%

(2) What was the percentage point increase in achieving Grade C Maths in School A from 2006 to 2009?
   (a) 15%   (b) 10%   (c) 20%   (d) 5%   (e) 25%

Question 7

The Deputy Head created the following table showing the number of pupils in each year group who had music lessons.

What is the percentage of pupils in all the year groups combined that have music lessons? Give your answer rounded to a whole number.

Year Group	Number of pupils	Number of pupils who have music lessons
7	92	10
8	101	18
9	105	14
10	96	13
11	102	11

(a) 21%   (b) 13%   (c) 19%   (d) 20%   (e) 22%

Question 8

The table below shows the total sales by a fashion retailer in London, Paris and New York

Total Sales	2008	2009	2010	2011
London shops (In Millions of £)	10.5	9.8	9.5	10.1
Paris shops (In Millions of Euros)	7.7	7.8	6.9	8.2
New York shops (In Millions of $)	15.1	14.3	14.6	14.9

(1) Assuming that in 2011 on average the exchange rates was £1 = 1.25 Euros and £1 = 1.6 US $. What were the total sales in 2011 for all three

cities in pounds sterling. Give your answer in pounds million to two decimal places.

(a) £24.92M   (b) £25.81M   (c) £28.82M (d) £25.97M (e) £27.25M

(2) What was the percentage increase in Sales in Paris from 2008 to 2009, giving your answer correct to 1 decimal place?

(a) 1.2% (b) 4.1%   (c) 2.1%   (d) 1.3%   (e) 2.2%

Question 9

An assistant meteorologist wants to convert a temperature of 22 degrees Celsius into Fahrenheit

The formula for converting the temperature from Celsius to Fahrenheit is given by:

$$F = \frac{9}{5}C + 32$$ (where C is the temperature in degrees Celsius). If the temperature is 22 degrees Celsius what is the equivalent temperature in Fahrenheit?

(a) 70.2 degrees Fahrenheit (b) 71.6 degrees Fahrenheit   (c) 81.6 degrees Fahrenheit   (d) 71.5 degrees Fahrenheit   (e) 73.3 degrees Fahrenheit

Question 10

Two managers and 12 employees go to France on a team building session. The exchange rate at the time they go is £1 = 1.3 euros. The employees change £50 each and the managers £100 each for themselves before going to France. When they come back the exchange rate is £1 = 1.25 euros. If they convert all their Euros left back to pounds they get back £28. How much in Euros did they spend altogether whilst in France?

(a) 102.5 euros (b) 1025 euros (c) 1025.6 euros (d) 1003.6 euros (e) 1005 euros

Question 11

The set of data below shows the result in a year 10 Geography test for 96 pupils. The marks are out of 10. The teacher wants to find the mean mark for this test. Give your answer to 1 decimal place.

Marks in Geography Test	No of pupils	No. of pupils × Geography marks	
1	1	$1 \times 1 = 1$	
2	5	$2 \times 5 = 10$	
3	12		
4	22		
5	27		
6	18		
7	7		
8	3		
9	1		
10	0		
Totals	96		

The mean mark is:

(a) 5.1   (b) 4.9   (c) 4.8   (d) 6.2   (e) 12.1

Question 12

In one school 140 pupils took maths GCSE exams. Both the percentage of pupils as well as the GCSE Grades obtained in maths is shown in the pie chart below.

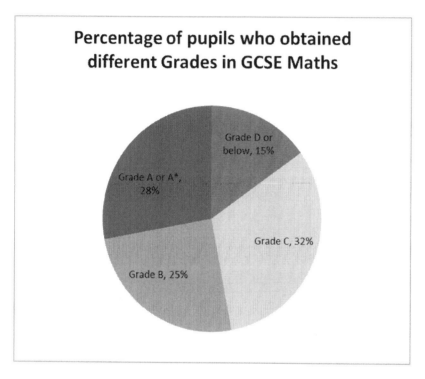

(1) What was the number of pupils who got Grade B?

(a) 36   (b) 32   (c) 40   (d) 35   (e) 27

(2) The percentage of pupils who got Grade C or above was:

(a) 86%   (b) 85%   (c) 87%   (d) 25%   (e) 92%

Question 13

The pie chart below shows the number of pupils who got a Grade C or better in English in four different schools

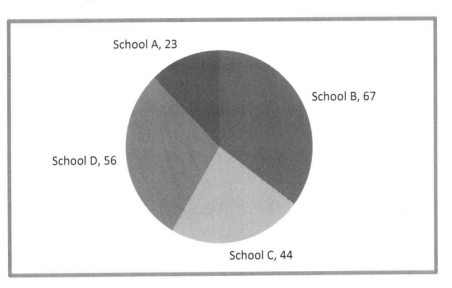

(1) The percentage of pupils who got Grade C or better in School C compared to all the other schools was approximately:

(a) 23.2%   (b) 24.5%   (c) 20.3%   (d) 21.2%   (e) 44.1%

(2) For grade C or better, the proportion of the total corresponding to School D was:

(a) $\frac{27}{95}$ (b) $\frac{28}{95}$ (c) $\frac{56}{95}$ (d) $\frac{28}{190}$ (e) $\frac{27}{190}$

Question 14

A teacher tells pupils that there will be a test in 4 weeks' time. She asks them to record their revision time over this period. Finally she shows the pupils the results of the maths test in relation to the time they spent revising in a scatter graph.

Scatter graph below shows the revision time in hours and resulting Maths marks

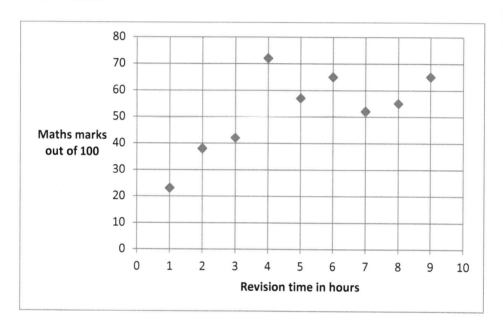

The number of pupils who get 50 marks or more in the test is:

(a) 7   (b) 6   (c) 8   (d) 3   (e) 9

Question 15

In a certain local authority the percentage of teachers and the years of teaching service completed before retirement was plotted in a cumulative frequency diagram.

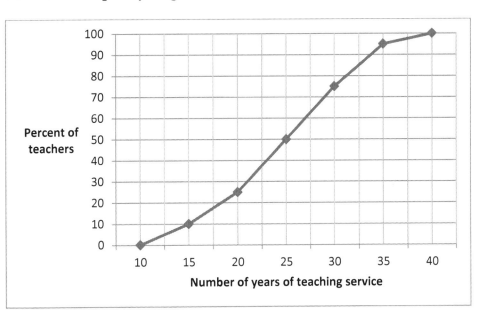

(1) The median for the number of years of teaching service is:

(a) 50   (b) 30   (c) 25   (d) 27.5   (e) 20

(2) The interquartile range for the number of years of teaching service is:

(a) 10   (b) 25   (c) 50   (d) 15   (e) 75

.

Answers to Test 4

Question 1

(1) Answer (d) 52.5%

Method: The mean % of those that earned £30,000 from 2008 to 2011 = (49 + 54 + 56 + 51)/4 = 210÷4 =52.5%

(2) Answer: (e) 50%

Method: Increase in percentage points from 2005 to 2011 = 17%

This increase of 17% was from 34%. To find the percentage increase we calculate $\frac{17}{34} \times 100 = \frac{1}{2} \times 100 = 50\%$ (Notice you can simplify $\frac{17}{34}$ to be equal to $\frac{1}{2}$ (cancel top and bottom by 17)

Question 2

Answer: (c) i.e. C, F & H

Method: Convert Test1 and Test2 into percentages first.

Hence in Test 1 and Test 2 the respective percentage marks for the pupils were:

Pupil A: 55% and 64%

Pupil B: 62.5% and 64%

Pupil C: 42.5% and 54%

Pupil D: 62.5% and 70%

Pupil E: 47.5% and 52%

Pupil F: 30% and 40%

Pupil G: 62.5% and 68%

Pupil H: 75% and 94%

So the pupils who had increased their marks by at least 10% from Test1 to Test2 were C, F and H

Question 3

(1) Answer (b) Hospital A

Method: The total admissions for the three days at the 4 hospitals were as follows: A =500, B = 440, C = 460, D = 290. Hence hospital A had the most admissions

(2) Answer (c) 33.33%

Method: Total admission on Sunday by the four hospitals = 90 + 100 +60 +20 =270. So percentage for Hospital A is $\frac{90}{270} \times 100 = \frac{1}{3} \times 100$ =33.33%

Question 4

(1) Answer (e) 60,000

Method: The number of Nook E-readers sold in Europe (UK, Germany & France) for March 2011 = (0.01 + 0.02 +0.03) million

= 0.06 million = 0.06 × 1000000 = 60,000

(2) Answer (c) Germany

Method: Combined Kindle & Ipad sales by country is USA = 3.5M, UK = 0.8m, Germany = 0.75M, France = 0.8m. Hence, the least sales were in Germany.

Question 5

(1) Answer (a) Company A

Method: To work out sales per employee in each country divide sales (£m) by number of employees:

Company A = £80,000; Company B =£ 60,000; Company C= £40,000 and Company D= £50,000. Hence Company A has the highest sales'

(2) Answer (d) £50,000

Method: 25% increase from £8m means the new sales are now £10M. Also the employees increased by 40, so the new number of employees are now 200. Finally dividing £10m by 200 we get £50,000

Question 6

(1) Answer (b) 7% (approximately)

Method: From the line graph in 2011, school A achieved approx. 27% success in achieving Grade C in Maths.

Similarly, school B achieved 34%. Hence the difference was 7%

(2) Answer (b) 10%

Method: From the line graph the percentage of pupils achieving the GCSE grade C success changed from 15% in 2006 to 25% in 2009. Hence this amounted to an increase in 10 percentage points.

Question (7)

Answer (b) 13%

Method: Total number of pupils = 496. Total number of pupils who have music lessons = 66. Hence percentage of pupils who have music lesson $=\frac{66}{496} \times 100$ = approx. 13%

Question (8)

(1) Answer (d) £25.97M

Method: Sales in £ sterling in 2011 were as follows:

London: £10.1M

Paris = 8.2 Million Euros, convert to sterling, 8.2÷1.25 = £6.56M

New York = 14.9 Million dollars, convert to sterling 14.9÷1.6
=£9.3125M. Adding up London, Paris & New York we get

10.1 + 6.56 + 9.3125 = £25.97M (to two decimal places)

(2) Answer (d) 1.3%

Method: increase in sales in Paris from 2008 to 2009 = 7.8 -7.7 = 0.1
million euros. Hence the percentage increase was $\frac{0.1}{7.7}$ × 100 = 1.3%

(1.3% is the answer to one decimal place)

Question 9

Answer (b) 71.6 degrees Fahrenheit

Method: Using the formula F= $\frac{9}{5}$ C +32 and substituting 22 degrees for
C we get F = $\frac{9}{5}$ × 22 +32 = 39.6 +32 = 71.6 degrees Fahrenheit

Question 10

Answer (e) 1005 Euros

Method: Total euros obtained initially by 2 managers = (£100×2×1.3) = 260

Total euros obtained by 12 employees= £50×12×1.3 = 780 euros

Grand total = 260 +780 = 1040 euros. However if they convert all their euros into pounds they get back £28. So at the given exchange rate (1.25 euros = £1), they must have had 1.25×28 euros left = 35 euros. Hence they must have spent (1040 − 35) euros altogether. That is 1005 Euros.

Question 11

Answer (c) 4.8

Method: Fill in the table as shown first:

Marks in Geography Test	No of pupils	No. of pupils × Geography marks	
1	1	$1 \times 1 = 1$	
2	5	$2 \times 5 = 10$	
3	12	$3 \times 12 = 36$	
4	22	$4 \times 22 = 88$	
5	27	$5 \times 27 = 135$	
6	18	$6 \times 18 = 108$	
7	7	$7 \times 7 = 49$	
8	3	$8 \times 3 = 24$	
9	1	$9 \times 1 = 9$	
10	0	$10 \times 0 = 0$	
Totals	96	460	

Now divide 468 by 96 to get the mean value. $460 \div 96 = 4.79166$ or 4.8 to 1 decimal place.

Question 12

(1) Answer (d) 35

Method: From the pie chart you can see that 25% got a grade B. Since there are 140 pupils altogether, this means 25% of 140 = 25. (50% of 140 =70, so 25% of 140 = 35)

(2) Answer (b) 85%

Method: From the pie chart it can be seen that 32% got a grade C, 25% got a grade B and 28% got grade A or A*. Hence the total percentage who got a grade C or above is 32% + 25% + 28% = 85%

Question 13

(1) Answer (a) 23.2%

Method: From the pie chart the total number of pupils who got a grade C or better in English in the four schools were: 23(School A) + 67(School B) + 44(School C) + 56(School D) = 190 pupils. In school C the percentage was: $\frac{44}{190} \times 100 = 23.2\%$ (to 1 decimal place)

(2) Answer (b) $\frac{28}{95}$

Method: Total number of pupils who made grade C or better in School D = 56. Hence the corresponding fraction compared to all schools is $\frac{56}{190}$, this simplifies to $\frac{28}{95}$

Question (14)

Answer: (b) 6

Method: From the scatter graph draw an imaginary horizontal line at 50 marks. The number of (points) pupils above this line corresponds to 6.

Question (15)

(1) Answer (c) 25

Method: The median is halfway up the vertical axis (frequency axis), in this case the percentage of teachers. Go horizontally from the 50% mark until it touches the curve and come down vertically to get 25 on the horizontal axis.

(2) Answer (a) 10

Method: The IQR (the interquartile range) is defined as the difference between the 75% mark (the upper quartile) and the 25% mark (the lower quartile). Again, going horizontally from these appropriate points until it touches the curve and coming down vertically we get 30 and 20 respectively. The difference between the two quartiles is equal to 10 years of service.

Practice Test 5   Word problems – 30 minutes (calculators allowed)

(1) Fatima and Louise have £350 between them. Louise has £80 less than Fatima. How much do they each have?

(2) The sum of three consecutive numbers is 54. What are the three numbers?

(3) The cost of a coat after a 20% discount is £85. What was its original price?

(4) The sum of two numbers is 36. One of them is 10 more than the other. What are the two numbers?

(5) The area of a rectangle is 162 m^2. The length of the rectangle is two times the width. What is the length and width of the rectangle?

(6) The total sales for Company A over two quarters were £2m. In the second quarter the sales were 50% more than the first quarter. What were the sales in the two respective quarters?

(7) The total number of employees in two Companies was 900. One of the companies had 250 employees less than the other. What were the number of employees in each company?

(8) John's annual salary is $\frac{3}{4}$ of Hilary's salary. Hilary's salary is twice Betty's. The total salary between them is $450,000. How much did each of them earn?

(9) The sum of two numbers is 30 and the difference between them is 8. What are the two numbers?

(10) Divide £90 between three people so that the second person will have 3 times as much as the first person. Also the third person has £15 less than the first person. How much do they each get?

(11) The sum of three consecutive odd numbers is 27. What are the three odd numbers?

(12) Divide $44 amongst three people so that the second two persons have half as much as the first person. How much do they each have?

(13) In a class of 31 students, a certain number of students go on a museum trip and the rest of the class go to an art gallery. The group that goes to the art gallery has 7 fewer students, how many students go to the museum?

(14) Divide £115 amongst three persons such that the second and the third person have the same amount and the first person has 3 times the second or third person. How much do they each have?

(15) The second number is $\frac{3}{4}$ of the first number. The sum of two numbers is 5.25. What are the two numbers?

Answers to Test 5

(1) Answer Fatima has £215 and Louise has £135

Method: Let the amount Fatima has be represented by x

Hence, Louise has x − 80. We know that the sum of the two amounts = £350. That is x + x − 80 =350. Simplifying, we get 2x − 80 =350. Now add 80 to both sides so we have 2x -80 +80 = 350 + 80. Which means 2x = 430, or x = 215. This means Fatima has £215 and Louise has £135 (Since Louise has £80 less than Fatima)

(2) Answer: The three consecutive numbers are 17, 18 and 19

Method: Let the first number be x. Hence the second consecutive number is x+1, and the third one x + 2. We know that the sum of these three numbers is 54. So x + x+1 + x +2 = 54, simplifying, we get 3x + 3 =54. Now subtract 3 from both sides to get 3x = 51. Dividing both sides by 3 we get x = 51÷3 =17.

Hence, the three numbers are 17, 18 and 19

(3) Answer: £106.25

Method: Let the original price be £x. This means x − 20% of x = 85

Or x − 0.2x = 85, which simplifies to 0.8x =85. Now divide both sides by 0.8. so we get x = 85÷0.8 = 106.25. Hence the original price is £106.25

(4) Answer: 13 and 23

Method: Let one of the numbers be x, hence the other number is x + 10. The sum of these two numbers is 36. So, x + x + 10 =36. This means 2x +10 = 36. Subtract 10 from both sides to get 2x = 26. Dividing both sides by 2, we get x =13. Hence the two numbers are 13 and 23

(5) Answer: width = 9m and length = 18m.

Method: Let the width =w and the length = 2w. We know that the area of a rectangle is length × width = 2w×w = $2w^2$. The area of the rectangle is given as $162m^2$. Hence, $2w^2$ = 162. Dividing both sides by 2, we get w^2 = 81. Hence w = $\sqrt{81}$ = 9. So the width is 9m and the length is 18m.

(6) Answer: £0.8M and £1.2M

Method: Let the sales in £m in the first quarter be x. The sales in the second quarter is 1.5x. We know that x + 1.5x = £2m, simplifying we get 2.5x =2, divide both sides by 2.5 to get x = 2÷2.5 = £0.8M and 1.5x = £1.2M

(7) Answer: Company A had 575 employees and Company B had 325 employees.

Method: Let the number of employees in Company A be represented by x. So x + x - 250 = 900, simplifying we get 2x − 250 = 900. Add 250 to each side to get 2x = 1150. Dividing both sides by 2, we get x = 575. Hence Company A has 575 employees and Company B has 575 - 250 = 325 employees.

(8) Answer: Hilary earns $200,000, John earns $150,000 and Betty earns $100,000

Method: Let Hilary's salary be x (in dollars). Hence, John's salary is $\frac{3}{4}$ x

Also, since Hilary earns twice as much as Betty, then Betty earns half of Hillary's = $\frac{1}{2}$x. Finally, we know that x + $\frac{3}{4}$ x + $\frac{1}{2}$x = $450,000, simplifying $2\frac{1}{4}$x = 450,000. Or, $\frac{9}{4}$ x = 450,000. This means 9x = 1,800,000 or x = 200,000. So Hilary earns $200,000, John earns $150,000 (three quarters of Hilary's amount) and Betty earns $100, 000 (half of Hilary's salary)

(9) Answers: 19 and 11

Method: Let the unknown numbers be x and y. This means x + y = 30, and x − y = 8, If we add the above two equations we get 2x = 38 (The y's cancel). Hence x = 19 and y = 11

(10) Answers: The first person has £21, second person has £63 and the third person has £6

Method: Let the first person have £x, this means the second person has £3x and the third person has £(x − 15). Now we know the sum total of these three persons is £90. This means x + 3x + x − 15 = 90. Simplifying, we get 5x − 15 = 90. This means 5x = 105 (add 15 to both sides). Now divide both sides by 15 to get x =21. Hence the first person has £21, second person has (3x as much) = £63 and the third person has x − 15 = 21 − 15 = £6

(11) Answers: The three odd numbers are 7, 9 and 11

Method: Let the first odd number be x, (Since odd numbers are 1, 3, 5, 7, 9, 11, ...) The next odd number is x + 2, and the one after that is x + 4. We know that the sum of three consecutive odd numbers is given as 27.

Hence, x + x+2 + x+ 4 =27, simplifying we get 3x + 6 = 27, subtracting 6 from both sides we get 3x =21. Finally, dividing both sides by 3 we get x = 7.

Hence the three consecutive odd numbers are 7, 9 and 11

(12) Answers: They each have $22, $11 and $11 respectively

Method: Let the amount the first person has be represented by x. This means the second and third person each have $\frac{x}{2}$. We know the total these three people have is $44. Hence x + $\frac{x}{2}$ + $\frac{x}{2}$ = 44. Simplifying, we get 2x = 44. Dividing both sides by 2, we get x = 22. So the first person has $22, the second and third person have $11 each.

(13) Answer: 19 students go to the Museum

Method: Let the number of students who go to the museum be x. From the information given we can write x + x − 7 = 31. Simplifying we get 2x − 7 = 31. Add 7 to both sides to get 2x = 38. Finally, divide both sides by 2 to get x =19. This is the number of students who go to the museum.

(14) Answers: 2nd & 3rd person each has £23 and the first person has £69

Method: Let the amount the second and third person have be £x each. This means the first person has £3x. The total is 3x + x + x = £115. Simplifying we get 5x = £115. Dividing both sides by 5 we get x = £23. So 3x = 69. This means the second and third person have £23 each and the first person has £69

(15) Answers: 3 and 2.25

Method: the sum of the two numbers are 5.25, let one of the numbers be x. Hence, $x + \frac{3}{4}x = 5.25$. Simplifying, we get 1.75x = 5.25, dividing both sides by 1.75 we get x = 3. So $\frac{3}{4}x = 0.75 X 3 = 2.25$. So the two numbers are 3 and 2.25.

Some basic reminders:

Even Numbers: All numbers that have 2 as a factor are even numbers.

Examples are: 2, 4, 6, 8, 10, 12, 14, 16

So, 168 is an even number as it can be divided exactly by 2.

Odd Numbers: Are all numbers that do not have 2 as a factor.

Examples: 1, 3, 5, 7, 9, 11, 13, 15, 17

So for example 81 is an odd number, as 2 is not a factor of 81.

Notice something interesting about odd numbers. The cumulative sum of consecutive odd numbers generates square numbers.

The first number is $1 = 1 X 1 = 1^2$

The sum of the first two numbers is $1 + 3 = 4 = 2 X 2 = 2^2$

The sum of the first three numbers is $1 + 3 + 5 = 9 = 3 X 3 = 3^2$

The sum of the first four numbers is $1 + 3 + 5 + 7 = 16 = 4 X 4 = 4^2$ and so on.

Multiples: These are simply numbers in the multiplication tables.

For example the multiples of 6 are 6, 12, 18, 24, 30, ...

Factors: A factor is a number that divides exactly into another number as for example, the number 2 in the case of even numbers.

3 is a factor of 9, as 3 goes exactly into 9.

15, has two factors other than 15 and 1. The two factors are 5 and 3, since both these numbers go exactly into 15.

Example: Find all the factors of 21. The factors are: 1, 3, 7 and 21

Prime Numbers: A prime number is a number that has two factors, the number itself and 1. Examples of prime numbers include 2, 3, 5, 7, 11, 13 and 17. So for example 23 is also a prime number since it has no other factor besides itself and 1.

Another example: Find the 3rd prime number after 11. The first prime after 11 is 13, the second prime is 17, and the third prime after 11 is 19.

Reciprocals:

The reciprocal of a number is 1 divided by the number. For example the reciprocal of 5 is $\frac{1}{5}$, the reciprocal of 13 is $\frac{1}{13}$ and so on.

Divisibilty by 9:

A number is divisible by 9 if its reduced digit sum is 9. Example: the number 18 can be reduced to 1+8 =9, so 18 is divisible by 9. 567 can be reduced to 5 +6 +7 =18 and 18 =1 + 8 =9. So, 567 is divisible by 9. 59049 can be reduced to 5 +9 +0 + 4 +9 = 27 and 27 = =2 +7 =9. Hence, the number, 59049 can be divided by 9.

Useful Websites for numerical reasoning tests

SHL tests:

http://www.shldirect.com/numerical.html

PSL/Kenexa tests:

http://www.psl.com/practice

Civil Service tests:

http://www.civilserviceprep.co.uk/public/samplecspexams.aspx

Kent University material

http://www.kent.ac.uk/careers/tests/mathstest2.htm

Printed in Great Britain
by Amazon.co.uk, Ltd.,
Marston Gate.